APPLICATIONS OF MORAL PHILOSOPHY

New Studies in Practical Philosophy
General Editor: W. D. Hudson

The point of view of this series is that
of contemporary analytical philosophy.
Each study will deal with an aspect of
moral philosophy. Particular attention
will be paid to the logic of moral discourse,
and the practical problems of morality.
The relationship between morality and
other 'universes of discourse', such as art
and science, will also be explored.

Published

R. M. Hare *Practical Inferences*
R. M. Hare *Essays on Philosophical Method*
R. M. Hare *Essays on the Moral Concepts*
R. M. Hare *Applications of Moral Philosophy*

APPLICATIONS OF MORAL PHILOSOPHY

R. M. HARE

*White's Professor of Moral Philosophy
in the University of Oxford*

UNIVERSITY OF CALIFORNIA PRESS

Berkeley and Los Angeles   1973

UNIVERSITY OF CALIFORNIA PRESS

Berkeley and Los Angeles, California

ISBN: 0–520–02232–7

Library of Congress Catalog Card Number: 74–187323

Printed in Great Britain

Second printing 1973

Contents

Acknowledgements

The Listener (Oct. 1955), by permission of the British Broadcasting Corporation. *La Philosophie Analytique*, Cahiers de Royaumont, no. IV (Editions de Minuit, Paris, 1959). T. H. B. Hollins (ed.), *Aims in Education* (Manchester University Press, 1964). *Elseviers Weekblad* (1964) and *Crucible* (1965). Research Students' Association, Australian National University, Canberra. P. Laslett and W. G. Runciman (eds), *Philosophy, Politics and Society*, III (Blackwell, Oxford, 1967). S. Verney (ed.), *People and Cities* (Fontana Books, London, 1969).

Editor's Foreword

This volume contains studies by an analytical moral philosopher of some practical moral problems. It gives the lie to those who accuse moral philosophers of being no longer interested in real moral issues. It reflects the author's wide range of interests and deep concern about what is happening within our society. All the issues discussed are of vital importance and call for moral choice on the part of all responsible persons. This collection of papers is interesting as an attempt at bridge-building between the theoretical concerns of the analytical philosopher and the practical questions which the moralist tries to answer. Can this bridge be built? Has moral philosophy anything to say which is of practical help to us in deciding what we ought to do? Not only philosophers but all intelligent men must find this question important and Professor Hare provides here examples of how it can be answered in the affirmative.

University of Exeter   W. D. HUDSON

Preface

I became a moral philosopher because I was troubled about practical moral questions; and from the time that I took up the subject I have (to help me in my theoretical work and for their own interest) continually done studies of such practical topics, some of which I have printed and some not. I have long wished to publish a collection of these, and am grateful to Dr Hudson and to Macmillan for encouraging me to do so; but by this time the papers available are far too numerous to go into one volume. I have therefore selected those which are in the best shape; the rest, mostly on medical, political or educational problems, will have to wait until I have caught up with their constantly changing subject-matter. None of the pieces here printed was aimed primarily at my philosophical colleagues, and they were written over a period of at least fifteen years; the reader must not, therefore, expect consistency of terminology or even of opinion, and I must warn students against trying by minute textual comparisons with these papers to shed light on the meaning of my more academic writings. Nevertheless the views here presented are grounded on my views in theoretical ethics, and, if allowance is made for some looseness of expression, consistent with them. I have, except for some omissions and minor editorial corrections, printed the papers in the form in which they were first published or broadcast. In the first volume of the set, *Practical Inferences*, I included a bibliography of my published writings, in which the contents of the other volumes can be discovered. Notes added in this edition are distinguished by asterisks; the original footnotes have numbers. I am grateful to the original publishers, who are identified in the footnotes, for giving their permission to reprint where necessary.

I shall be satisfied if some who read these papers are led to

think that philosophical thought can help us towards the
solution of practical problems, and if a few of these join the
increasing number of philosophers who are actually trying to
show how it can be done.

Corpus Christi College,   R. M. HARE
Oxford
1971

I   Can I Be Blamed for Obeying Orders?

Many people, if asked for the distinctive feature of present-day British philosophy, would say that it lies in the peculiar attention which we tend to pay to the study of language. Perhaps most British philosophers would agree that the study of language, in some sense, is a very potent philosophical tool; and many would say that it is *the* philosophical method – that any problem which is properly philosophical reduces in the end to an elucidation of our use of words. Criticisms of this approach to philosophy are frequently made by those who have not practised the sort of method we use, and therefore do not understand either what the method is, or how fruitful it can be. It is alleged that we are turning philosophy away from matters of substance to trivial verbal matters (as if it were a trivial matter to understand the words we use); and it is also sometimes said that we are to be contrasted unfavourably in this respect with the great philosophers of the past.

The purpose of these talks is to indicate, by means of two examples taken from political philosophy, that both these criticisms arise from misunderstandings of the nature of philosophy in general and of our kind of philosophy in particular. The point could have been made by means of a general discussion about philosophical method; or it could have been made by taking examples out of the works of famous philosophers, and showing how much kinship there is between their methods of argumentation and ours. But I thought it better to take two practical problems of political morality – problems which exercise us currently, or ought to – and to show how a

This was the first of two talks given in Germany, and later on the B.B.C. Third Programme, in 1955 under the title 'Ethics and Politics'. The second talk is not reprinted here, since it has been replaced by no. 7 of this volume. Both talks were published in *The Listener* for October 1955.

great deal of light can be shed on these by an understanding
of the words used in discussing them: an understanding of the
sort which it is the purpose of contemporary moral philosophy
to achieve. None of the things I shall say will be original;
indeed, it is part of the point of these talks that they are not
original: I am merely translating into a new, and I think
clearer, idiom things which have been said by great philosophers
of the past, and thereby showing that the new idiom is a vehicle
for philosophy as it has always been understood.

In the first of these talks I shall discuss a problem which
arises frequently in wartime and in connexion with war-crimes
trials. The thesis is sometimes maintained that a soldier's duty
is always to obey orders; and this is often brought forward as a
defence when someone is accused of having committed some
atrocity. It is said that, since it is a soldier's duty to obey his
orders, and he is liable to blame if he disobeys them, we cannot
consistently also blame him if in a particular case he obeys
them – even though the act which he has committed is of
itself wrong. We may blame his superiors who gave the orders,
but not the man who carried them out. Others, in opposition
to this, maintain that the individual is always responsible for
his own acts.

Can the study of moral language shed any light on this
problem? I want to maintain that it can; and the way I shall
do this is by exhibiting the formal features of the problem, as
they arise out of the logical properties of the words used in
discussing it. I wish to show that these formal features are
common to a large range of questions which are not at first
sight similar, and that the key to the whole matter is a purely
linguistic and logical observation made a long time ago by
Hume.

The formal features of this problem are brought out extremely
clearly by Kant in a famous passage,* in which he is arguing
that we have to make our own moral judgements, and cannot
get them made for us, without any decision on our part, by
God. Suppose that I am commanded by God to do something.
The Bible is full of stories where this is said to have happened.
Can I without further consideration conclude that I ought to
do it? Kant argued (rightly) that I cannot – not without
further consideration. For it does not follow automatically, as

* *Groundwork*, 2nd ed., p. 92 (tr. Paton, *The Moral Law*, p. 104).

it were, from the fact that God wills me to do something, that I ought to do it. From the fact that God wills me to do something, I can only conclude that I ought to do it if I am given the additional premiss that God wills that and that only to be done, which ought to be done. This additional premiss is one which indeed Christians all accept, because they believe that God is good; and part of what we mean by saying that God is good is that he wills that and that only to be done which ought to be done. But we have to assume this, if we are to pass from the fact that God wills us to do something to the conclusion that we ought to do it. So we can indeed, as it were, get out of making the particular moral decision as to whether we ought to do this particular thing, by putting it on the shoulders of God; but only at the cost of having to make for ourselves a more general moral decision, that we ought always to do what God commands (the very fundamental, crucial decision that is made when anyone decides to become, or to remain, an adherent of the Christian or some other religion). This more general moral judgement obviously cannot, without arguing in a circle, be shuffled off our shoulders in the same way.

Yet, if we do not assume that God is good, the only conception we have left of him is one of power without goodness – one, as Kant picturesquely puts it, compounded of lust for glory and domination, together with frightful ideas of power and vengefulness; and to make our duty the obedience to the will of such a being would be to adopt a highly immoral morality. We might rather be inclined to approve of disobeying an evil God, as Shelley portrays Prometheus doing, however appalling the consequences.

I want you to notice that this argument does not depend on its being God's will in particular upon which it is sought to base morality. The same argument would apply were we to substitute for 'God' the name of any other person whatever, divine or human. Kant is here making use of a principle in ethics which was, so far as I am aware, first stated by Hume. The actual passage is worth quoting, both because it is rightly held to be one of the two or three most important observations in moral philosophy, and because it illustrates very well my thesis that the subject-matter of philosophy is the use of words. Hume says:

In every system of morality, which I have hitherto met with,
I have always remark'd, that the author proceeds for some

time in the ordinary way of reasoning, and establishes the being of a God, or makes observations concerning human affairs; when of a sudden I am surpriz'd to find, that instead of the usual copulations of propositions, *is*, and *is not*, I meet with no proposition that is not connected with an *ought*, or an *ought not*. This change is imperceptible; but is, however, of the last consequence. For as this *ought*, or *ought not*, expresses some new relation or affirmation, 'tis necessary that it shou'd be observ'd and explain'd; and at the same time that a reason should be given, for what seems altogether inconceivable, how this new relation can be a deduction from others, which are entirely different from it. But as authors do not commonly use this precaution, I shall presume to recommend it to the readers; and am persuaded that this small attention wou'd subvert all the vulgar systems of morality. . . . (*Treatise*, III I i)

It is easy to apply this canon of Hume's to our example. The proposition 'X's will is, that I do A' (where X is any person whatever and A is any act whatever) is a proposition of fact, an 'is'-proposition. It does not matter who X is; in Kant's example it was God; but it might be some human ruler. From this 'is'-proposition the 'ought'-proposition 'I ought to do A' cannot be derived. The first proposition states a mere fact, a fact about what someone wills that I do. From this fact no moral proposition follows. Only if we are given the *moral* premiss, 'X wills that and that only to be done, which ought to be done' or 'Everything which X wills to be done, ought to be done' can we, from this, in conjunction with the premiss 'X's will is, that I do A', conclude that I ought to do A. This is all right, because we have added to our factual minor premiss a moral major premiss; and from the two together we can infer a moral conclusion; but not from the factual minor premiss alone.

In the example with which I started, X was God. But I wish to discuss the first and most celebrated example of a philosopher who thought that moral decisions could be made on his subjects' behalf by a ruler, namely Plato. Plato thought that, just as there are experts in riding and in other skills, so there ought to be experts in morals. All we had to do, in order to solve all moral problems, was to get such an expert, make him our philosopher-king, and leave him to decide for us what was right and what was wrong. He would make the laws, and we, by obeying them, could be absolutely certain of living morally blameless lives. This programme has an obvious and immediate appeal. For moral problems are difficult and tormenting; how fortunate it would be if we could leave them, like problems of engineering, to somebody who could solve them for us! To get rid of one's moral problems on to the shoulders of someone else – some political or military leader, some priest or commissar – is to be free of much worry; it is to exchange the tortured responsibility of the adult for the happy irresponsibility of the child; that is why so many have taken this course.

The flaw in this arrangement is that we could never know whether the philosopher-king really was a philosopher-king. Plato himself admits that his ideal republic might degenerate. The maintenance of the republic depended on the correct calculation of the famous Platonic Number,* which was used for determining the correct mating-season to produce the philosopher-kings of the next generation. If the Number were miscalculated, a person might be made ruler who did not really possess the required qualifications. Suppose that we are inhabitants of a Platonic republic, and are ordered by our so-called philosopher-king to do a certain act. And suppose that we are troubled about the morality of this act; suppose that it is the act of torturing some unfortunate person. It is perfectly true that if our ruler is a *true* philosopher-king, then, *ex hypothesi*, he knows infallibly what is right and what is wrong, and so we cannot do wrong to obey him. But the question is: Can we be sure that he is the genuine article? Can we be sure that they did not miscalculate the Number a generation ago, so that what we have at this moment is not a philosopher-king, but the most wicked of tyrants masquerading as one?

We can tell whether a man is a good man, or, specifically, whether a king is a good king, only by considering his acts. So that it is no use saying of *all* our ruler's acts, 'He is the philosopher-king, and the philosopher-king can do no wrong; therefore each and every act of his must be right'. For this would be to argue in a circle. It is only if we are satisfied that his acts are right that we can be satisfied that he is a good king. Therefore if he commands us to perform what looks like an atrocity, the only thing we can do is look at the individual act and say, 'What about this very thing that he is commanding

* *Republic*, 546 c.

me to do now? Could a good man command anyone to do this?' That is to say, we have to make up our own minds about the morality of the king's acts and orders.

Governing is different from engineering in an important respect. The engineer as such is concerned with means only; but government involves the choice both of means and of ends. If you know no engineering, you have to get the best engineer you can to build your bridge; but the engineer is not the man who decides that there shall be a bridge. Therefore, we can say to the engineer, 'We want a bridge just here'; and leave him to build it. We judge him by his success in bringing about the end which we have set him. If his bridge falls into the river, we do not employ him again. Rulers also often have to find means to ends which are agreed upon. For example, it is recognised that it is a bad thing if large numbers of people starve through being unable to get employment; and we expect our rulers nowadays to see to it that this does not happen. The means to this end are very complicated, and only an economist can understand them; but we are content to leave our rulers to employ competent economists, understand their prescriptions as best they can, choose between them when, as often, they conflict, and generally do their best to realise the end of full employment without impairing any other of the ends which we also wish to realise. But in government someone has to decide on the ends of policy. In a democracy this is done by the voters. They do it in part explicitly and in advance, by choosing between parties with rival policies; but in the main they do it implicitly and by results, by turning out of office those parties who do not achieve the ends which the voters desire.

In Plato's republic it was different. The people were supposed to be entirely ignorant both about means and about ends; the rulers decided on both. And if the ruler decides both on the means and on the end, one cannot judge him as one judges the engineer. For one can say to the engineer, 'You were told to produce a bridge that stood up to the weather, and your bridge has been blown into the river'. But if we have not told our ruler to do anything – if we have just left it to him to decide on the ends of political action – then we cannot ever accuse him of not fulfilling the purposes which we intended him to fulfil. He can always say, 'I did what I thought good, and I still think it good'. This is the decisive point at which Plato's analogy between the ruler and the expert breaks down. The expert is an expert at getting something done, once it has been decided *what* is to be done. Plato's philosopher-king was supposed to do not merely this – he was supposed not merely to perform a task, but to decide what the task was to be. And this is a thing that cannot be left to experts; it is the responsibility of all of us.

If it is true that we cannot leave the moral problems about political ends to a Platonic philosopher-king, then it is still more obviously true that we cannot leave them to any ordinary human superior. As I said at the beginning, we often hear it said by someone who is accused of a war-crime – for example of killing some innocent people in cold blood – 'I did it on the orders of my superior officers; I am not morally guilty'. If the superior officers could likewise be found and charged they would say the same thing, until we got back, perhaps, to some high-up ruler who initiated in some very general terms some policy whose detailed execution involved the slaughtering of the innocents. But how can the orders of somebody else absolve *me* from moral responsibility? It may indeed absolve me from legal responsibility: that is a different matter, and depends on the law that is in force. But if we are speaking of a matter of morals, surely the man who is ordered to do such an act has to ask himself whether it is morally right for him to do it. It cannot follow, from the 'is'-proposition that X orders me to kill these people, that I ought to kill them. The people who order these crimes, and I who execute them, are accomplices, and share the responsibility.

In many cases, admittedly, a person in such a position can plead that he is acting under duress; he, or his family, will be shot if he does not obey orders. We do tend to excuse a man in such a position, or at any rate to blame him less. Why we do so is also a matter upon which the study of moral language can shed a good deal of light; but I have no time to discuss it now. Let us exclude duress from the argument by assuming that the subordinate knows that his superiors will not find out whether he has obeyed orders or not: let us suppose that he is the head of a mental home who has been ordered to poison all incurables, and that he himself does the classification into curables and incurables.

Up to a certain point, indeed, a person in this position can plead ignorance of fact; his superiors, no doubt, have access to more information than he has, and can foresee consequences of the omission to murder these people which might not be known to the person who has to perform the act. Up to a point a subordinate can say, 'I cannot see the whole picture; I must be content to leave the formulation of policy to my superiors, whose job it is to know what the consequences would be of various alternative policies, and to make a choice between evils'. But the point must in the end come when a subordinate has to say, 'Any policy which involves my doing this sort of thing (for example, slaughtering all these people in cold blood) must be a wicked policy, and anyone who has conceived it must be a wicked man; it cannot therefore be my duty to obey him'. To decide just when this point has been reached is one of the most difficult problems in morals. But we must never banish from our minds the thought that it might be reached. We must never lose sight of the distinction between what we are told to do and what we ought to do. There is a point beyond which we cannot get rid of our own moral responsibilities by laying them on the shoulders of a superior, whether he be general, priest or politician, human or divine. Anyone who thinks otherwise has not understood what a moral decision is.

2   Reasons of State

1. *Acts and their Consequences*

Last autumn, a few days after the invasion of Egypt, I was asked, as we all were at Oxford, to sign a protest which declared that the British and French action was, among other faults, morally wrong. I signed the protest, because I *did* think the invasion morally wrong; but not without some misgiving; because, of the many people who were going round at the time saying that the invasion was morally wrong, I did not find a single one who could give me a clear account of the reasons why he thought this. Another thing that troubled me was that in all discussions of the subject much was made of the contrast between morality and expediency: it was said that our two governments had 'sacrificed morality to expediency'; yet I never met anybody who could give me an explanation of this distinction which I could begin to understand. So, although I signed the protest, I did not stop worrying about these questions; and since they illustrate very well some of the deepest problems in moral and political philosophy, I thought it worth while to write out in as clear a way as possible what I thought about them. These two talks are the result.

Right at the beginning we run up against the main difficulty. Is it possible to make moral judgements about political actions at all? It is sometimes said that it is not. For example, it is generally thought morally wrong to tell lies; but sometimes, it is said, if you are a diplomat, it would be unthinkable to give a true answer to an awkward question. If, for example, you were accredited to a stronger power which was thought to be considering invading your own country, what would you say if you were asked a question such that a true answer to it would reveal, and an evasion would suggest, that the armed forces

An address given in Germany, and later on the B.B.C. Third Programme, in 1957.

of your own country were in no fit state to resist an attack? Would you tell a lie? I know of a man who gave up a promising career in the Foreign Service because he realised that he might have, in the course of his diplomatic duties, to do things which, if he did them in private life, he would consider immoral. Diplomacy and politics generally, it might be said, are a dirty business, and the man who wants to keep his hands clean ought not to have anything to do with them. But if this view is taken by everybody, we shall lack politicians and diplomats; or if, as is more likely, it is taken only by all *honest* people, we shall lack *honest* politicians and diplomats. And what should we do without them?

By some such reasoning as this, people often come to the conclusion that it is in principle mistaken to judge political actions by moral criteria. Reasons of state, it is said, can, and in crucial cases ought to, override moral considerations. Sometimes it is even said that great political decisions are too *important*, or too far-reaching in their consequences, to allow them to get mixed up with morality; the clear-headed and far-sighted statesman will make up his mind unconfused by moral scruples. Political decisions have to be made on political grounds; moral principles are a luxury that only the humble private citizen can afford.

In favour of this immoral-sounding position, one other very plausible argument may be adduced. The private citizen, when he makes a moral decision, is often deciding only for himself; the sacrifices, that is to say, which he makes for the sake of acting rightly are his own sacrifices. This is not, of course, universally true; for a man with dependants (for example a father with a large family or an employer with a lot of workers) is often in a position in which, if he acts on some moral principle, he will be sacrificing, in the cause of right action, the welfare of others. But the contrast with political decisions still has some force: the statesman is, on the whole, much *more* often in a position in which, if he acted on some generally accepted moral principle, he would be saving his own soul at the expense of other people's bodies. In such circumstances he may say, 'The people have put me here to look after their interests, not to play at being a moral paragon; I should be failing in my *duty* to them if I did not do whatever will promote those interests, even if it isn't very nice morally'. The word 'duty' has some sense, surely, in such a remark; but what is this sense?

Should a statesman make all his decisions on the simple criterion, 'Would this policy promote the interests of the people of my country?' Is the answer, perhaps, that the statesman is the representative of his people's consciences as well as of their interests? They have a duty to do all that they can to see that he does, on their behalf, what is right; and he has a duty to co-operate in this, and indeed to go as far ahead of public opinion as he dares. That is why informed public discussion, public protests, and even stronger action are so important; they help to keep statesmen straight. But suppose a statesman knows that his people's consciences are in a somnolent condition; suppose that, if he does what he thinks morally right at the expense of what they conceive to be their interests, he is likely to be turned out of office. That does not mean that he has necessarily *got* to follow some morally wrong policy; he can always do what he thinks right, and face the immediate political consequences. But here the original difficulty recurs again. If the question at issue is an important one, so that it dwarfs every other consideration, no doubt he ought to stick to his moral guns. But if it is a matter of less importance, he may say to himself, 'Politics is the art of the possible'; he may think that he would be doing wrong, in *this* situation, if he left the government in the hands of others more unscrupulous than himself, when, perhaps, more important decisions are in the offing. This is, needless to say, a type of argument which has often been used to support actions which should never be condoned. But *sometimes* it is a reasonable argument.

We have, then, two extreme positions, each of which has some plausibility as against the other, but neither of which, we feel, can be right. One of them says that moral principles – the same principles – are binding on statesman and private citizen alike; it is indeed much more difficult for the statesman to abide by them; but the person who is daunted by this difficulty ought not to become a statesman. The other position says that morality applies only to the decisions of private life, and that political decisions are to be judged by political standards only. How are we to decide between these two views, or find a compromise or synthesis between them?

It may help us to consider some *logical* features of the language which we use in expressing moral principles. This is, perhaps, the only contribution that the philosopher, as such, can make to the solution of this problem; it is also a contribution which only he can make, and which needs making. People sometimes say that a moral principle ought to be unconditional; that no conditions or *ifs* should be attached to the fulfilment of the principle. This might be used as an argument for the position that it makes no difference to the bindingness of a moral principle that the person who is called upon to obey it happens to be a politician. One should absolutely *never* tell lies, for example; there are absolutely *no* conditions under which one may do so.

Let us examine this position more closely. There is obviously something wrong with saying that moral principles must be literally *un*conditional. For any moral principle is bound to state *some* conditions under which something is to be done or avoided. This follows from the fact that a principle is always expressed by a universal sentence of some sort, and any universal sentence turns out on analysis to contain a conditional clause. These are logical truths. For example, the principle 'Never tell lies' says that *if* any statement would be a lie, we are not to make it; the principle 'Always keep promises' says that *if* any act would be, or would involve, the breaking of a promise, we are not to do it. Try making a moral principle literally *un*conditional, and you will see what I mean. Try, for example, taking away the condition from the principle about promise-keeping. It says, in its present form, that if any act would be, or involve, the breaking of a promise, we are not to do that act. If we remove the conditional clause, what we shall have left is the principle 'Do no acts whatever'. And since omissions are also, for the purposes of this argument, acts, this principle is logically impossible of fulfilment.

But if I am right about this (if *some* condition is attached to any moral principle) we cannot lay down without further reflection that the *only* conditions affecting the morality of a political act are those in which it resembles the acts of private people. It may be that the circumstances of a person making a political decision are different, in some morally relevant particulars, from those of a private person making what in some obvious respect is a superficially similar decision. And this is indeed usually the case. I think we should most of us agree that what determines the morality of an act is, in large measure, its effects on other people. But it is characteristic of political actions that they affect far more other people than do most ordinary private actions. It follows that the situation of a statesman is, when he makes a decision, different in a morally relevant respect from the situation of a private person, in that his actions have widespread effects on other people, which he has to take into account. Thus, if the effect of keeping a promise would be to precipitate a war in which vast numbers of people would be killed, this might make us say that *in these circumstances* it would be our moral duty to break the promise, even though in most circumstances promises ought to be kept. On the other hand, perhaps there are circumstances in which a promise to make war ought to be both made and kept. These difficulties are the stuff of which political decisions are made.

And so both parties to the dispute which I have been discussing are wrong. The person who says that moral principles do not apply at all to political decisions makes one mistake: he supposes that, since there is a new factor which affects political decisions, this factor puts them outside morality altogether. But what it actually does is to introduce new *moral* considerations alongside the old ones, to be balanced against them. It is still a moral decision, but a more complicated and difficult one. The person who says that the moral principles which we apply in private life ought to be carried over unchanged into politics makes a different mistake. He is ignoring a factor in the situation which is morally relevant – the fact that a political decision has effects which a private decision does not have, or not to the same degree. He is like – to adapt a famous example of Plato's* – the man who in private life thinks that you ought always to keep a promise, even when it was a promise to give back a gun to a person, and the person has gone mad and wants to go round shooting people with it. His moral principles are *too* simple.

There is another point which will certainly have occurred to you while I have been talking – a point which is bound to crop up sooner or later when one discusses this problem. It is a point about the distinction between an act and its consequences. It is sometimes said that in making a moral judgement on an act that has been done, or in deciding whether we ought, morally,

* *Republic*, 331.

to do some act that is proposed, we must pay attention only to the nature and quality of the act, and entirely disregard the consequences. People who think this could not be expected to agree with the view which I have just put forward, with its emphasis on the effects of our actions on other people. *Fiat justitia, ruat caelum* is their motto. I think that most people, who at the time of Suez said that morality had been sacrificed to expediency, had some such distinction as this in mind. The idea was that Sir Anthony Eden, in deciding to join the French in this adventure, was doing something that he knew to be wrong in order that good results might be brought about. He was, as they say, making the end justify the means.

As is well known, the difficulties begin when we start trying to distinguish between the things called 'the nature and quality of the act' on the one hand, and 'the consequences of the act' on the other. What is an act? Here is another point at which one of these 'verbal trivialities' of philosophy has a profound bearing on the way in which we assess a political policy. What, for example, is the *act* whose nature and quality we are judging if we condemn Eden's (or the government's) act in invading Egypt? Is it the uttering by some cabinet ministers of verbal instructions to their subordinates, and is everything that followed a *consequence* of the uttering of these words? Or does the act include the actual dropping of bombs and landing of troops and killing of Egyptians – were these acts of soldiers and airmen in some sense acts of the British government? If so, does the act include such further consequences as may have been brought about? Could we say of Eden that *he shook* the Anglo-American alliance, or that *he impaired* Britain's reputation for plain dealing, or that *he reduced* our influence for good in the Middle East or in the United Nations? Or, if you are on the other side in politics, could you say that *he prevented* further Soviet intervention in Syria and Egypt, and thus lessened the danger of a world conflagration; or that by separating the combatants *he struck a blow* for the preservation of law and order? If one can, without linguistic impropriety, say things like this, can one not also say that all these various things that Eden did were acts of his – and acts, moreover, that were morally relevant in judging his policy? For if all we had to judge was the utterance of words by cabinet ministers, and all these other things were ruled out as morally irrelevant because they were *consequences*, what would there be left to judge? What happened at the vital cabinet meeting was wrong, or right – whichever it was – *because* it had these consequences, and was intended to have them.

To take another example: it has been said that Mr Truman ought not to have dropped the first atomic bomb, because it was murder and that should have absolutely excluded the act from the start, without any consideration of the consequences of dropping it or not dropping it. But how are we to delimit Truman's act? Was it the giving of an order to a subordinate? Or was it having the bomb dropped from an aeroplane? Did it include, as well as this, the killing of the people the bomb was dropped on? If so, did it also include the frightening of the Japanese government into surrender, or the consequent saving of Allied and Japanese lives? We could certainly say, without linguistic impropriety, 'Truman, by dropping the bomb, saved more lives than he destroyed'. I am not now arguing about whether this was in fact the case, or even about whether Truman had good reason for thinking that it would be the case. All I am doing is attacking the philosophical theory that a distinction can be drawn between an act and its consequences in such a way that the consequences become morally irrelevant. Surely, in this case, there is no way of drawing this distinction.

But really I do not see how such a distinction can *ever* be drawn. For my acts (what I *do* in the appropriate sense of 'do') are what I cause to happen. My causing something to happen is always an act, and if, in addition, the thing is intentionally caused to happen, it is an intentional act and can be morally judged as such. From this it follows that if there is any consequence of my act which I intend should be a consequence of it, the bringing about of that consequence is also an intentional act of mine. So, in the example I have given, if the killing of the inhabitants of Hiroshima was an intended consequence of Truman's order, he intentionally killed them, and the killing of them was an intentional act of his; and similarly, if the saving of the other lives was an intended consequence of his order, that too was an intentional act of his. Neither of these consequences of his order can be ruled out as morally irrelevant just because they are *consequences*.

I think that the conclusion of this argument is unavoidable. In making a political decision, as in making any other, we have to consider, in so far as we can predict them, the total effects of the alternative choices, and then single out, from among these total effects, those which are morally relevant. It is our moral principles which tell us *which* effects are morally relevant and which are not. The basic mistake of the position which I have been attacking is to suppose that there can be two processes, one of first singling out the morally relevant features, and the other of later applying our moral principles to those features. But, in fact, the morally relevant features of a situation are simply those to which our moral principles, whatever they are, refer. It is simply a question of asking, 'Of all the things which I should be doing if I did a certain thing, are there any which I ought not to do? And if, as may well be the case in a complicated situation, to do *any* of the things that are open to me would be a breach of some moral principles, what am I to do about it?'

2. *Principles and their Application*

I have rejected both of two opposite views about the relation of morality to politics. The first was that politics are outside morality; political decisions have to be judged by their own, political standards; morality is a matter for private life. The second was that the moral principles which we use in private life can be applied without further reflection to political decisions. The conclusion which I tried to establish was that moral principles *are* applicable to political decisions, but that, because political decisions are very far-reaching in their effects upon other people, and so many different factors are involved, making them is a very complicated matter; and that therefore we cannot expect to be able always to guide our political decisions by the comparatively simple moral principles which suffice for the most part in private life.

I am going to discuss now two opposite ways in which philosophers often try to cope with the problem posed by the complexity of political decisions. I shall, as before, maintain that they are both wrong, and shall suggest a synthesis between them. And though I shall be speaking in the main of political decisions, I do not want you to think that what I say applies only to them; for even private decisions are often more complex than some philosophers seem to suppose; and, in so far as they are complex, the remedies for complexity may be the same.

The first of the remedies which I am going to reject is often proposed by the same sort of people as hold a position which I argued against in my previous talk: the position that the simple moral principles which we use in everyday decisions of private life can be carried over without reflection into politics. The remedy is, in fact, an extension of that position. The suggestion is sometimes put in the form that moral principles have by nature to be absolutely *general*. The sort of 'absolutely general moral principles' which are quoted by people of this school are principles like the ones I discussed before: 'Never tell lies'; 'Never commit murder'; 'Always keep promises'. I think that these examples give a clue to what these people mean by that tricky word 'general'. They mean that *conditions* should not be attached to the fulfilment of the principles. The reason why this is supposed to be a remedy for the complexity of political decisions is that if the basic principles of morality are general like this, and if we know what they are, they will *rule out* for us, absolutely, certain courses of action; and this may simplify our choice considerably. If, for example, we can say that to do a certain thing would be to tell a lie, or break a promise, or do a murder, then, *without any further reflection*, we can rule out that course of action, whatever else we should thereby find ourselves doing. And such a simplification of political choices has an obvious attraction.

Now I argued that it is logically impossible for a moral principle to be literally *un*conditional. A moral principle that was literally *un*conditional would be vacuous; it would not tell us to do or to abstain from anything in particular. So the position which I am discussing cannot, without reducing it to absurdity, be taken as implying that *no* conditions can be attached to moral principles. What, then, does 'general' mean? Consider for a moment the two principles 'Never tell lies, ever' and 'Never tell lies except when it is necessary in order to save an innocent life'. Would a representative of this view say that the first of these principles was more general than the second, or wouldn't he? The second principle ('Never tell lies except when it is necessary in order to save an innocent life') contains a condition which the first does not; for the first says, 'Never tell lies, ever'. This is not to say that the first principle is absolutely *un*conditional; for it too contains a condition; it says that *if* any statement would be a lie, we are not to make it. But, given that both principles contain conditions, is the shorter one more general? Now I can think of only two answers that might be given to this question. It might be answered that the principle with the extra clause was inferior in generality. We might say, 'It is less general, because it applies in fewer cases; according to it you only have to avoid telling lies when this wouldn't cause the deaths of innocent people'. Or, on the other hand, it might be answered that the longer principle is not inferior in generality, because both of the principles apply to *anybody* who comes under the conditions specified, and anybody *might* come under these conditions.

If a representative of the view which I am attacking takes this second line, he will, I think, have to admit that even the most complicated principle, with any number of conditions attached to it, can be 'absolutely general' in the sense required by his position; for the principle will still apply to *anybody* who falls under these conditions. If this is what he says, then I have no further quarrel with him, for he is saying exactly what I want to say myself, though I would express it differently. But, of course, if the man takes this line, he cannot claim that he is making the application of moral principles to politics any simpler; for if principles are allowed to have as complicated conditions attached to them as you please, without ceasing to be 'absolutely general', we shall no longer have those delightfully simple moral principles which are supposed by this school of thought to be an infallible guide through the political maze.

But suppose that, instead of this answer, it is answered that the principle 'Never tell lies unless it is necessary in order to save an innocent life' *is* less general than the principle 'Never tell lies, ever'. If this is what is said, then it becomes clear that what these people mean by 'generality' is just *simplicity*. Granted that all principles, for the logical reason that I have just given, have to contain *some* conditions, the general principles which these people are advocating have to contain as few and as simple conditions as possible. So let us take it that this is what they want to say, and see whether this proposal does offer us a remedy for the complexity of political decisions.

I think that it will at once be clear that it does not. For if situations are complicated, as they are, you cannot be sure that you will be able to apply simple principles to them without further reflection. We have, in fact, the problem of *applying* our moral principles to the individual case. This is a problem with all principles, but especially with simple ones. I think you can see the problem most easily if you consider what happens if these simple principles happen to conflict with one another in some particular case. For it certainly seems that they *may* conflict. Suppose that I am in Hungary and I am asked by the A.V.O. what a friend of mine did during the revolution, and what he actually did was something they would shoot him for. Ought I to tell them the truth? I myself should tell a lie in these circumstances. And I should not think that in telling it I was doing wrong. For although to tell it would be an act of a kind which in nearly all circumstances *would* be wrong, namely lying, in *these* circumstances it would be the right thing to do.

This is a relatively simple example. But what we feel inclined to say about it applies with even greater force to the more complex decisions of political life. If it is the case that, where moral principles conflict, I may have to make an exception to one of them in favour of another, I can never say, just because one principle seems to apply to a particular case, that I can proceed to act on that principle without further reflection; for further reflection might, if I exercised it, reveal that there was another principle (for example, loyalty to friends who have done nothing wrong) which also applied to the case; and still more reflection might make me decide that this other principle is the one which should be obeyed as it stands, and that the first one ought to have an exception made to it. So these simple, general principles are no substitute for reflection, which, in the case of the man who actually has to make the choice, may well be agonising. One should have firm general principles; but their function is not to absolve us from reflection – even from reflection about the principles themselves.

To these remarks two important qualifications must be made. The first is that there is not always *time* for much reflection. The statesman has to act one way or the other, and learn from his mistakes. This is not an argument against reflection; on the contrary, it is an argument for reflecting as much as possible

on actual and possible cases, while there is time, and so fore-
arming ourselves with well-thought-out principles against
likely contingencies. This is the chief importance, for the
statesman, of the study of history. And how important it is, too,
that there should be informed public discussion of political
issues, and that the machinery of government should be so
arranged that those who have to make the choices have time
to attend to and reflect on these discussions! By far the greater
number of wrong decisions are made because people don't
arrange their business so as to give themselves time to think.

The other qualification I wish to make is that, although the
simple moral principles which we all naturally think of when the
word 'principles' is used are not immune from amendment in
the light of reflection on particular cases, we ought not to be
too ready to amend them. For these copy-book maxims are
principles which have, in the great majority of cases, stood the
test. For example, we cannot say *a priori* – by abstract reasoning
– that there are *no* cases in which the statesman ought to break
promises or tell lies, but we can say, *a posteriori* – because of the
way things are – something a little less sweeping but more
solid: that these cases are very rare indeed, and certainly far
rarer than opportunist politicians deceive themselves into
thinking. Statesmen who have done these things without over-
whelming reason have hardly ever achieved anything much
that was creditable either morally or in any other way. The
same applies to other moral principles such as 'Don't be
vindictive'; 'Respect other people's interests'; 'Never use
violence if you can possibly avoid it'; and so on. It is very seldom
even expedient to ignore these principles.

I have no time to say any more about the first of the suggested
remedies for the complexity of political choices. I now turn to
the second, which seems its exact opposite. The second remedy
might be described, in a familiar phrase, as that of 'judging each
situation on its merits'. Now of course this phrase, as it is
commonly used, draws attention to an important fact about
moral decisions, especially in politics – indeed to the very fact
about them on which I have been dwelling so long, namely
that, since they are complicated, you cannot make them
without reflection on the peculiarities of the particular case.
But, taken in an extreme way, the maxim that one ought to

judge each case on its merits might seem to mean that one has
no use for principles at all. And this would be a bad doctrine
for politicians to get hold of.

This doctrine solves, or seeks to solve, the problem of the
complexity of politics in a completely different way from the
suggestion which I considered first. Instead of saying, 'There
are a few simple rules, armed with which you can face the
tangles of political life', it says, 'You don't need to fuss yourself with rules; take each situation as you come to it, and
you'll see what to do'. Now I think you will notice what is
wrong with this second remedy if you consider what is involved
in the phrase 'judging each situation *on its merits*'. For if, when
we have considered a particular situation, we decide that,
morally speaking, the right thing to do is X and not Y, this
must be because of *something about* doing X as opposed to Y –
because of some great moral drawback that doing Y has, so
that we ought to do X, even though, perhaps, X too may have
drawbacks which in this case have to be endured. And to
think this is already to signify that you are going on a principle –
the principle that this *something about* Y is something which in
these circumstances ought to be avoided even at the cost of
those other things which would be brought about by doing X.
And this is a principle which *may* have an application outside
these particular circumstances – whether it *has* such an application will only be determined by further reflection about such
other circumstances as we seek to apply it to. This reflection,
both in the original situation and in others, is directed towards
singling out those features of the situations which are morally
relevant; and, as I have said before, to say that certain features
of situations are morally relevant is already to form moral
principles. Part of what we mean by an experienced statesman
is, a man who has been in plenty of difficult political situations
and has learnt something from them. This means that, whatever he actually did in those situations, he has reflected on
what he ought to have done, and so acquired principles which
may guide him when he meets new difficulties. These principles
will certainly be complicated and tentative ones – for one ought
never to stop learning; and they will probably be impossible to
do justice to by any formulation in language. That is why there
can be no primers of statesmanship; one has to think over
the lives of the great statesmen of the past, and by reflection

elicit the principles which guided them to such achievements as they have to their credit. The remedy which I have been attacking gains some plausibility from the fact that great statesmen often seem to act intuitively, without invoking any obvious principle. But this does not show that *no* principle is being followed – only that it is a complicated and probably inarticulate principle which can be learnt by studying the man's actions and in no other way. If the people whom I am attacking were right, there would be no difference between the beginner in politics and the experienced statesman; both would come entirely unprepared and without principles to each new decision, and make it on the merits of the situation with equal chances of success. But in fact what distinguishes the old hand is that he has learnt something in the course of his life – namely his political principles, which, if he is a good man as well as a good politician, will include moral principles.

As I come to the end of these talks, it may seem to you that I haven't done what I set out to do at the beginning, namely to distinguish between morality and expediency. Actually, I started by casting doubt on this distinction; and what I have said has strengthened the doubt. For I have talked about morality in a way that makes it very difficult to distinguish it from at any rate one kind of expediency. Both morality and expediency are matters of considering the consequences of the actions between which we have to choose, and choosing that action which has the consequences which we think, in the circumstances, we ought to bring about. What, it may be asked, is the difference if we add a word and say 'which we *morally* ought to bring about'? The answer is, I think, that, when we think of it as a *moral* decision, we have to consider, not merely what consequences would be *in our own interest*, or in that of our *own* country, but what consequences ought to be chosen by *anybody* placed in such a situation. It means that we have to consider the effects of our actions on other people and other countries, as well as upon ourselves, and, having imaginatively placed ourselves in their position, think whether we can still say that we ought to do what our own interest prompts us to do. We have to consider, in Kant's phrase, whether we can will the maxim of our action to become a universal law. Really the fundamental difference is not between morality and expediency; it is between a narrow national self-interest and public spirit. Both can be called kinds of expediency; for both aim at some good, and the expedient is what is conducive to good. But the first is an immoral kind of expediency, aiming only at the good of the agent and his country; whereas the second is a kind of expediency which is coextensive with morality.

Now when I agreed to sign this paper declaring that the British and French invasion of Egypt was morally wrong, what I meant was not anything so simple as what most people seem to have meant. It may have been morally wrong for the reasons which were commonly given, and to which I have already referred. But – far more important, as it seems to me – it was morally wrong in the same sort of way as it would be morally wrong to drive at sixty miles an hour through a crowded market-place. The action was so foolish, so regardless of the consequences which were almost certain to follow, as to amount to a case of criminal recklessness. It was wrong *because* it was inexpedient. It did no good, and much harm, to the Egyptians, the Israelis, the Hungarians, the world in general, and the British not least. But since my reasons for this judgement are not philosophical ones, I shall not give them now. I only want to make the point that an act which harms *everyone* is almost certain to be morally wrong, if it is deliberate – for one morally ought not to harm other people when there is no compensating good.

Many of you, I am sure, will disagree strongly with the political views which I have just expressed about Suez. Since this is a philosophical, not a party-political broadcast, I shall not try to defend them. I expressed them only in order that people may not say, as they often do say, that philosophers don't *care* about politics. I always lose my temper when they say this – for I happen to care rather a lot. When people make this accusation, what they really mean is that philosophers ought to be using their philosophy to *prove* political conclusions, so that ordinary voters, instead of making up their own minds about political issues, can just ask a philosopher. But it is not the function of philosophy to make up people's minds for them. It aims only at *understanding*; and its initial move is often to show that we do not understand what we think we understand. That is why it is so unpopular.

3   Function and Tradition in Architecture

'Function' is one of the key words of present-day writing about architecture, and functionalism the most prominent architectural orthodoxy of the present time. Has the word got a distinct meaning? My question was prompted by the reading of a book – a very beautiful book – called *The Functional Tradition in Early Industrial Buildings*, written by Mr J. M. Richards and illustrated with many excellent photographs by Mr Eric de Maré and others. The book is a joy to have in one's hands and is well worth its considerable price. Here we have pictures of the London Docks; naval dockyards; railway, canal and other warehouses and sheds; mills and factories of all sorts from the late eighteenth century to the early nineteenth; breweries; and, as sauce to this meat, the better-known beauties of windmills, water-mills, oast-houses, canal bridges and aqueducts, and a final chapter which conducts us swiftly over a wider span of time, from a medieval tithe barn to a modern power-station cooling tower.

And we are convinced – though I did not require convincing – that such buildings can be beautiful. Mr de Maré's camera, like a modern Claude-glass, could make a picture out of almost anything; but it isn't just that. Dark and Satanic though some of these buildings are (the word used in the book is 'grim') they have a power to compel the eye (if one lets it be compelled); and, when we have finished the book, we have learnt something about what makes buildings beautiful.

But it is very hard indeed to say just *what* we have learnt. Mr Richards has a doctrine which may be summarised – I hope not unfairly – as follows. Functionalism is often thought of as a modern, indeed as a revolutionary creed; but this is quite wrong. Modern functionalists are only the latest successors in

B.B.C. Third Programme talk, 1959.

what Mr Richards calls 'The Functional Tradition', which goes back through the buildings pictured in this book to medieval castles and beyond. So let present-day functionalists realise that they are not revolutionaries, but respectable members of the establishment. Let them settle down. 'After the revolution', he says, 'comes consolidation, depending on the creation of a vernacular language. . . . How can this better be done than by striving to carry on the functional tradition which inspired the anonymous vernacular of these early industrial buildings.'

There is much truth in all this; but in order to discover *what* truth, it is necessary to examine more closely what Mr Richards means. Since the best way to do this is to push his doctrine around a bit, I hope that I may be forgiven if I do just that, even if the short time available compels me to do it somewhat roughly (in both senses of the word).

First of all 'tradition'. This *should* mean, 'something *handed down* from one generation to another'. A way of doing things is not traditional if one thinks it up for oneself. In what sense, therefore, can we say that the men who built these early factories were following a tradition? Well, in many cases (like *all* builders of their time, even the most extravagantly unfunctional ones) they used traditional *materials*, and availed themselves of traditional *crafts*. The other main traditional influence was stylistic; many of these builders tried to give aesthetic tone to their buildings (and succeeded remarkably well) by incorporating conventional Georgian details which they had learnt from the 'great architecture' of the preceding period.

But is Mr Richards entitled to speak of a *functional* tradition? For if these buildings are functionalist, what makes them so seems at first sight to be also just what makes them *different* from what they would have been like if their builders had just followed tradition – not the pediments and fanlights, not the traditional brick and stone, but the long horizontal weavers' windows and the cast iron. Unless functionalism makes a difference to the way people build, the doctrine becomes vacuous, as marking no distinction; and this is, indeed, a disease to which this doctrine, like so many other doctrines in aesthetics, is highly susceptible, as we shall see.

Could we perhaps almost say that what is traditional about these buildings is not functionalist, and what is functionalist is not traditional? Take, for example, that perfectly lovely picture of the Albert Dock, Liverpool, built in 1845 to the design of Jesse Hartley, the dock surveyor. The cornices and quoins which frame the warehouses are traditional, but not especially functional; on the other hand (as Mr Richards points out) the rows of windows equally spaced and sized are functional but not traditional. The fronts of the warehouses are supported on arches and cast-iron doric columns, making a very beautiful pattern. Such columns are a very common feature of industrial architecture of this period; they had been used earlier by Telford for docks in London. The fact that the columns are doric is due to tradition; that they are of cast iron is due to inventiveness in response to need. Almost *no* feature of the picture is both functionalist and traditional. And we might in the same way 'take apart' many more of the pictures in this book – and, for that matter, many buildings that are not in the book, such as the Iron Bridge near Broseley (one of the finest examples of functional buildings).

It is clear, therefore, that we can't, if we are going to give any plausibility to Mr Richards' doctrine, take the word 'tradition' as referring to the handing down of actual techniques or stylistic traits. It must refer to something a great deal more elusive – an attitude or habit of mind, perhaps. But the question now arises, Was this attitude *handed down* (whether consciously or not), or did it only *recur spontaneously* whenever people set themselves to put up buildings with a predominantly practical purpose? If Mr Richards had given us the historical basis for an answer to *this* question, we should all be in his debt. Probably the answer is that sometimes functionalism in buildings is the result of a traditional attitude, but sometimes it arises spontaneously; if so, then the 'Functional Tradition' is probably not so continuous as Mr Richards seems to imply.

But what is the 'functionalist' attitude of mind? Here again we have to push the word around before we discover much about its meaning. 'Functionalism' is, as Mr Richards rightly says, a word whose meaning 'has been continually distorted and misunderstood' (perhaps, we might add, because the propagators of the doctrine have themselves not been entirely clear what they meant by it). This he seeks to remedy by the following definition. It is, he says, 'the principle that the process of designing a building begins with a close analysis of the needs it is to serve. It has as its object [he goes on] the fulfilment of such needs as logically and economically as possible.' The first thing that strikes us about this definition is that the word 'begins' is in the indicative mood. Surely Mr Richards cannot mean 'does begin'; for if architects always do begin the process of designing a building in the way that he specifies, then they are *all* functionalists; but in this way, again, the word loses its meaning, because it no longer serves to mark a distinction. Of course Mr Richards means, not 'begins' but 'ought to begin' or 'should begin'. He is, that is to say, making a normative judgement (or rather attributing such a judgement to functionalists, who no doubt include himself). He is commending those architects who do begin by considering the needs a building is to serve, and condemning those who don't.

This may seem a pedantic point; but it isn't. For as soon as we see that this is a normative judgement, we begin to ask, What *kind* of normative judgement? Is it for example a *moral* judgement? This is not so unplausible as it sounds; but I don't think that it can be *only* moral advice that Mr Richards intends. If architects sin *qua* architects, it must be by putting up bad buildings. So the question shifts and becomes, What sort of judgement are we making when we call a building a good or a bad building? The answer is, of course, that it may be of many *different* sorts; and therefore the obscurities of Mr Richards' intention deepen. For we can commend a building for different kinds of virtues: either because it is aesthetically pleasing, or because it fulfils well the needs it was designed for, or because it is economical to erect and maintain – to name three important qualities of good architectural designs. The problem of understanding what is meant by functionalism is the problem of knowing whether, on the one hand, it is a doctrine about how to achieve one or another of these virtues in buildings independently of the rest, and if so which; or whether, on the contrary, it is a doctrine about the *relation between* these virtues – a doctrine, for example, that the pursuit of one of them (say the fulfilment of needs) somehow conduces to the achievement of another (say beauty).

To illustrate the complexity of the problem, let me give a few examples, out of many, of what Mr Richards' doctrine might mean. It might be just a piece of advice about how to achieve buildings that fulfil the needs that they are being designed to fulfil. His prescription can then be put in the form of a hypo-thetical imperative like those of Kant: 'If you want your buildings to serve well the needs they are to serve, you should begin with a close analysis of those needs' – a piece of advice which is almost, if not entirely, platitudinous. We might bring in economy into a judgement of the same form: 'If you want your buildings to serve well the needs they are to serve, *and* to be economical, you should begin with a close analysis of those needs, and of the means of satisfying them economically'. In short, 'If you want practical buildings, you should think about how to produce them before you think about anything else' – excellent, if somewhat obvious, advice!

If this were the *whole* of Mr Richards' advice, then it would contain nothing whatever about aesthetics, and would be pretty unexciting. For how could it be denied that *if* what you want is practical buildings, that is what you ought to think about? But I know that this is not all Mr Richards means, because, directly after the passage I quoted, he goes on, 'Its [the building's] aesthetic character is created as part of the same process; nor does the exercise at every stage of personal preferences and aesthetic taste, which is inherent in all archi-tectural activity, in any way invalidate the functional basis of modern architecture'.

Now what does he mean by 'is created as part of the same process'? He might simply mean that the process of designing a building *begins* (or ought to begin) with a close analysis of the needs it is to serve, but it also *includes* (or should we say, as before, 'ought to include'?) a consideration of the building's aesthetic character. This boils down to the somewhat jejune doctrine that if you want a practical building that is *also* aesthetically pleasing, you ought to think about practical questions first, but oughtn't to forget to think about aesthetics some time, as part of the same process of design. But this doctrine, again, is so platitudinous that I hesitate to attribute it to Mr Richards.

Let's try, then, to think of something else he might mean. I think that he *may* mean that there is a *relation* between the aesthetic and the practical aspects of design – a relation more intimate than that of being both parts of the same process. Does he mean, for example, that *being aesthetically pleasing* is one of the needs that a building has to fulfil; and that, accordingly, an analysis of the needs will necessarily include a consideration of the building's appearance? If this is what he means, then we have to ask further questions. Who decides what needs the building is to fulfil? The client perhaps. But if so, the doctrine, as I have just interpreted it, is by no means universally true. For in many cases the client may, in specifying his requirements, say nothing about the building's appearance. He may even say 'To hell with the appearance! I want a factory that makes money and doesn't cost too much.' This may, indeed, have been the case with some of the buildings illustrated in the book, though certainly not all of them. And I don't think Mr Richards wants to say that, if the client demands beauty, the architect ought to provide it, but if not, it doesn't matter.

But suppose we waive this objection and say categorically that *being aesthetically pleasing* just *is* one of the needs that a building has to fulfil (needs, shall we say, of the public, if not needs of the client). But then we run into a more serious objection. If to be a functionalist is to seek to fulfil *this* need along with the others, then pretty well all architects will have to be called functionalists, differing only in the emphasis they place on the separate parts (aesthetic and practical) of a building's function. And thus we shall encounter yet again our old bogey, the reduction of the term 'functionalist' to vacuity by leaving nothing for it to distinguish between. And if it is said that after all it is *hard* to distinguish between the aesthetic and the practical, because there are so many borderline cases (as indeed there are) then this, besides being a dubious argument, leaves us in no better position.

If we reject all these possible interpretations of Mr Richards' meaning, we are driven back on to the following. Does he perhaps mean that there is a *causal* relation between the thought which an architect gives to the function of a building and the aesthetic quality of the resulting building? By this I do not mean – for this would land us yet again in triviality – that if the building is put up to the architect's design, what the building looks like will depend on what goes into the design. This, of course, is true of all buildings whatever, and on all theories whatever except palpably false ones. I mean that if, by his thought about a building's function, an architect succeeds in fulfilling *well* the needs it serves, then, by some unexplained causal link, this will tend to *make* the building a more beautiful one than it would be if it served the needs less well. Is this what Mr Richards means by 'is created as part of the same process'? It is certainly a view which has been held by people calling themselves functionalists.

If this view is to be at all plausible, it must not be put in too strong a form. It would be absurd to suggest that the successful fulfilment of a building's function is the *only* factor determining its beauty. The Chinese Room at Claydon, for example, would be less, not more, beautiful if its exuberant *chinoiseries* had been made more restrained in the interests of economy, durability and the comfort of the guest. Nor can it be claimed, as a general rule, even that, all other things being equal, a building which fulfils its function well must be aesthetically better than one which fulfils it less well. For there may be no aesthetic difference at all between the two buildings; for example, if the thermal insulation of one is much worse than that of the other, and if therefore the fuel bills of one owner are twice as high as they should be, his building is worse at fulfilling its function; but the buildings may *look* exactly the same. And, conversely, two functionally identical buildings might differ in aesthetic quality because of the colours chosen for painting them. Many of the buildings illustrated in the book, indeed, owe a great deal of their beauty to the way in which they are painted; but, with certain obvious exceptions, the colour of paint makes no difference to function. So it certainly looks as if the aesthetic and practical merits of a building can vary independently.

What, then, is the truth in functionalism? If I had to answer this question, I would say, 'A small truth – perhaps a dull truth – but a very important one not to forget'. It is a truth, not about what is *obligatory* upon architects, but about what is *possible* for them. It is possible to pay close attention – even predominant attention – to the practical function of a building without thereby detracting from its aesthetic qualities. Perhaps we might even be a little bolder. In so far as an architect, in designing a building, keeps his aesthetic aims working *with* his practical aims, instead of letting them get at loggerheads, he is the more likely to achieve both these aims. And it is *possible* for him to do this. The reason is – and this is perhaps the chief lesson to be learnt from the book – that our appreciation of beauty is, or can become, something much more flexible and accommodating than most people think. By stretching our aesthetic muscles we can learn to like – and like very much – buildings which struck us at first as ugly or uninteresting. This is what Mr de Maré's camera teaches us; and it is a lesson which obviously has applications to other arts besides architecture. It follows that an architect can safely pursue function in the certainty that a building whose shape is determined by its function can yet take on a beauty appropriate to that shape. It will not inevitably do so; the architect has to think about the appearance as well. Yet function is not a hindrance but (provided that it is treated as such) a help.

Some architects of past generations may have acted on the principle that if one pays too much attention to the practical purpose of a building, it is likely to be ugly; that if one wants a building to look well, one has *got* to concentrate on its appearance almost from first to last. Even if no *great* architect ever thought this, a great deal of people, clients and critics as well as architects, talked as if they did. Against this attitude, functionalism was a fully justified protest – a protest which has done immeasurable good and still needs making. It needs making, not only because few architects even now, especially in England, are practical-minded enough; but because we have not yet fully explored the exciting aesthetic possibilities offered by new materials and methods of construction. And when the old styles were getting thoroughly stale and stuffy, the functionalists let some fresh air into the architectural profession, and set it free to think about the needs of its clients more than about academic stylistic quarrels. So we must certainly applaud them, for all the imprecision of their language; and if they can call in Telford and Jesse Hartley and the other dock- and factory-builders as posthumous allies, good luck to them! If those old men were to come to life again and read Mr Richards' book, how pleased they would be – but also how mystified!

4 'Nothing Matters'

Is 'the Annihilation of Values' something that could happen?

I

I want to start by telling you a story about something which once happened in my house in Oxford – I cannot remember now all the exact details, but will do my best to be accurate. It was about nine years ago, and we had staying with us a Swiss boy from Lausanne; he was about 18 years old and had just left school. He came of a Protestant family and was both sincerely religious and full of the best ideals. My wife and I do not read French very well, and so we had few French books in the house; but those we had we put by his bedside; they included one or two anthologies of French poetry, the works of Villon, the confessions of Rousseau and, lastly, *L'Etranger* by Camus. After our friend had been with us for about a week, and we thought we were getting to know him as a cheerful, vigorous, enthusiastic young man of a sort that anybody is glad to know, he surprised us one morning by asking for cigarettes – he had not smoked at all up till then – and retiring to his room, where he smoked them one after the other, coming down hurriedly to meals, during which he would say nothing at all. After dinner in the evening, at which he ate little, he said he would go for a walk. So he went out and spent the next three hours – as we learnt from him later – tramping round and round Port Meadow (which is an enormous, rather damp field beside the river Thames on the outskirts of Oxford). Since we were by this time rather worried about what could be on his

The original English version of a paper contributed to the Cercle Culturel de Royaumont in 1957. The French version is published with a report of the subsequent discussion and the other proceedings of the Cercle's conference, under the title *La Philosophie Analytique* (Cahiers de Royaumont, no. IV, Editions de Minuit, 1959).

mind, when he came back at about eleven o'clock we sat him down in an armchair and asked him what the trouble was. It appeared that he had been reading Camus's novel, and had become convinced that *nothing matters*. I do not remember the novel very well; but at the end of it, I think, the hero, who is about to be executed for a murder in which he saw no particular point even when he committed it, shouts, with intense conviction, to the priest who is trying to get him to confess and receive absolution, 'Nothing matters'. It was this proposition of the truth of which our friend had become convinced: *Rien, rien n'avait d'importance.*

Now this was to me in many ways an extraordinary experience. I have known a great many students at Oxford, and not only have I never known one of them affected in this way, but when I have told this story to English people they have thought that I was exaggerating, or that our Swiss friend must have been an abnormal, peculiar sort of person. Yet he was not; he was about as well-balanced a young man as you could find. There was, however, no doubt at all about the violence with which he had been affected by what he had read. And as he sat there, it occurred to me that as a moral philosopher I ought to have something to say to him that would be relevant to his situation.

Now in Oxford, moral philosophy is thought of primarily as the study of the concepts and the language that we use when we are discussing moral questions: we are concerned with such problems as 'What does it mean to say that something *matters*, or *does not matter*?' We are often accused of occupying ourselves with trivial questions about words; but this sort of question is not really trivial; if it were, philosophy itself would be a trivial subject. For philosophy as we know it began when Socrates refused to answer questions about, for example, what *was* right or wrong before he had discussed the question '*What is it to be* right or wrong?'; and it does not really make any difference if this question is put in the form 'What is rightness?' or 'What is the meaning of the word "right"?' or 'What is its use in our language?' So, like Socrates, I thought that the correct way to start my discussion with my Swiss friend was to ask what was the meaning or function of the word 'matters' in our language; what is it to be important?

He very soon agreed that when we say something matters or is important what we are doing, in saying this, is to express concern about that something. If a person is concerned about something and wishes to give expression in language to this concern, two ways of doing this are to say 'This is important' or 'It matters very much that so and so should happen and not so and so'. Here, however, I must utter a warning lest I be misunderstood. The word 'express' has been used recently as a technical term by a certain school of moral philosophers known as the Emotivists. The idea has therefore gained currency that if a philosopher says that a certain form of expression is used to *express* something, there must be something a bit shady or suspicious about that form of expression. I am not an emotivist, and I am using the word 'express' as it is normally used outside philosophical circles, in a perfectly neutral sense. When I say that the words 'matters' and 'important' are used to express concern, I am no more committed to an emotivist view of the meaning of those words than I would be if I said 'The word "not" is used in English to express negation' or 'Mathematicians use the symbol "+" to express the operation of addition'.

Having secured my friend's agreement on this point, I then pointed out to him something that followed immediately from it. This is that when somebody says that something matters or does not matter, we want to know *whose* concern is being expressed or otherwise referred to. If the function of the expression 'matters' is to express concern, and if concern is always *somebody's* concern, we can always ask, when it is said that something matters or does not matter, 'Whose concern?' The answer to these questions is in most cases obvious from the context. In the simplest cases it is the speaker who is expressing his own concern. If we did not know what it meant in these simple cases to say that something matters, we should not be able to understand what is meant by more complicated, indirect uses of the expression. We know what it is to be concerned about something and to express this concern by saying that it matters. So we understand when anybody else says the same thing; he is then expressing his own concern. But sometimes we say things like 'It matters (or doesn't matter) to *him* whether so and so happens'. Here we are not expressing our own concern; we are referring indirectly to the concern of the person about whom we are speaking. In such cases, in contrast to the more simple cases, it is usual to give a clear indication of the person whose concern is being referred to. Thus we say,

'It doesn't matter *to him*'. If we said 'It doesn't matter', and left out the words 'to him', it could be assumed in ordinary speech, in the absence of any indication to the contrary, that the speaker was expressing his *own* unconcern.

II

With these explanations made, my friend and I then returned to the remark at the end of Camus's novel, and asked whether we really understood it. 'Nothing matters' is printed on the page. So somebody's unconcern for absolutely everything is presumably being expressed or referred to. But whose? As soon as we ask this question we see that there is something funny, not indeed about the remark as made by the character in the novel, in the context in which he is described as making it (though there is something funny even about that, as we shall see), but about the effect of this remark upon my friend. If we ask whose unconcern is being expressed, there are three people to be considered, one imaginary and two real: the character in the novel, the writer of the novel, and its reader, my Swiss friend. The idea that Camus was expressing his *own* unconcern about everything can be quickly dismissed. For to produce a work of art as good as this novel is something which cannot be done by someone who is not most deeply concerned, not only with the form of the work, but with its content. It is quite obvious that it mattered very much to Camus to say as clearly and tellingly as possible what he had to say; and this argues a concern not only for the work, but for its readers.

As for the character in the novel, who thus expresses his unconcern, a writer of a novel can put what sentiments he pleases in the mouths of his characters – subject to the limits of verisimilitude. By the time we have read this particular novel, it seems to us not inappropriate that the character who is the hero of it should express unconcern about absolutely everything. In fact, it has been pretty clear right from the beginning of the novel that he has not for a long time been deeply concerned about anything; that is the sort of person he is. And indeed there are such people. I do not mean to say that there has ever been anybody who has literally been concerned about *nothing*. For what we are concerned about comes out in what we choose to *do*; to be concerned about something is to be disposed to make certain choices, certain efforts, in the attempt to affect in some way that about which we are concerned. I do not think that anybody has ever been *completely* unconcerned about *everything*, because everybody is always doing something, choosing one thing rather than another; and these choices reveal what it is he thinks matters, even if he is not able to express this in words. And the character in Camus's novel, though throughout the book he is depicted as a person who is rather given to unconcern, is depicted at the end of it, when he says these words, as one who is spurred by something – it is not clear what: a sense of conviction, or revelation, or merely irritation – to seize the priest by the collar of his cassock with such violence, while saying this to him, that they had to be separated by the warders. There is something of a contradiction in being so violently concerned to express unconcern; if nothing *really* mattered to him, one feels, he would have been too bored to make this rather dramatic scene.

Still, one must allow writers to portray their characters as their art seems to require, with all their inconsistencies. But why, because an imaginary Algerian prisoner expressed unconcern for the world which he was shortly to leave, should my friend, a young Swiss student with the world before him, come to share the same sentiments? I therefore asked him whether it was really true that nothing mattered to him. And of course it was not true. He was not in the position of the prisoner but in the position of most of us; he was concerned not about nothing, but about many things. His problem was not to find something to be concerned about – something that mattered – but to reduce to some sort of order those things that were matters of concern to him; to decide which mattered most; which he thought worth pursuing even at the expense of some of the others – in short, to decide what he really wanted.

III

The values of most of us come from two main sources; our own wants and our imitation of other people. If it be true that to imitate other people is, especially in the young, one of the strongest desires, these two sources of our values can be seen to have a common head. What is so difficult about growing up is the integration into one stream of these two kinds of values. In the end, if we are to be able sincerely to say that something matters for *us*, we must ourselves be concerned about it; other people's concern is not enough, however much in general we may want to be like them. Thus, to take an aesthetic example, my parents may like the music of Bach, and I may want to be like my parents; but this does not mean that I can say sincerely that I like the music of Bach. What often happens in such cases is that I *pretend* to like Bach's music; this is of course in fact *mauvaise foi* – hypocrisy; but none the less it is quite often by this means that I come in the end to like the music. Pretending to like something, if one does it in the right spirit, is one of the best ways of getting really to like it. It is in this way that nearly all of us get to like alcohol. Most developed art is so complex and remote from what people like at the first experience, that it would be altogether impossible for new generations to get to enjoy the developed art of their time, or even that of earlier generations, without at least some initial dishonesty.

Nevertheless, we also often rebel against the values of our elders. A young man may say, 'My parents think it matters enormously to go to church every Sunday; but *I* can't feel at all concerned about it'. Or he may say, 'Most of the older generation think it a disgrace not to fight for one's country in time of war; but isn't it more of a disgrace not to make a stand against the whole murderous business by becoming a pacifist?' It is by reactions such as these that people's values get altered from generation to generation.

Now to return to my Swiss friend. I had by this time convinced him that many things did matter for him, and that the expression 'Nothing matters' in his mouth could only be (if he understood it) a piece of play-acting. Of course he didn't actually understand it. It is very easy to assume that all words work in the same way; to show the differences is one of the chief ways in which philosophers can be of service to mankind. My friend had not understood that the function of the word 'matters' is to express concern; he had thought mattering was something (some activity or process) that things did, rather like chattering; as if the sentence 'My wife matters to me' were similar in logical function to the sentence 'My wife chatters to me'. If one thinks that, one may begin to wonder what this activity is, called mattering; and one may begin to observe the world closely (aided perhaps by the clear cold descriptions of a novel like that of Camus) to see if one can catch anything doing something that could be called 'mattering'; and when we can observe nothing going on which seems to correspond to this name, it is easy for the novelist to persuade us that after all *nothing matters*. To which the answer is, ' "Matters" isn't that sort of word; it isn't intended to *describe* something that things do, but to express our concern about what they do; so of course we can't *observe* things mattering; but that doesn't mean that they don't matter (as we can be readily assured if, as I told my friend to do, we follow Hume's advice and "turn our reflexion into our own breast"*)'.

There are real struggles and perplexities about what matters most; but alleged worries about whether anything matters at all are in most cases best dispelled by Hume's other well-known remedy for similar doubts about the possibility of causal reasoning – a good game of backgammon.** For people who (understanding the words) say that nothing matters are, it can safely be declared, giving but one example of that hypocrisy or *mauvaise foi* which Existentialists are fond of castigating.

I am not saying that no *philosophical* problem arises for the person who is perplexed by the peculiar logical character of the word 'matters': there is one, and it is a real problem. There are no pseudo-problems in philosophy; if anything causes philosophical perplexity, it is the philosopher's task to find the cause of this perplexity and so remove it. My Swiss friend was not a hypocrite. His trouble was that, through philosophical naïveté, he took for a real moral problem what was not a moral problem at all, but a philosophical one – a problem to be solved, not by an agonising struggle with his soul, but by an attempt to understand what he was saying.

I am not denying, either, that there may be people who can sincerely say that very little matters to them, or even almost nothing. We should say that they are psychologically abnormal. But for the majority of us to become like this is a contingency so remote as to excite neither fear nor attraction; we just are not

* *Treatise*, III 1 i.   ** *Treatise*, I 4 vii.

made like that. We are creatures who feel concern for things –
creatures who think one course of action better than another
and act accordingly. And I easily convinced by Swiss friend that
he was no exception.

So then, the first thing I want to say in this talk is that you
cannot annihilate values – not values as a whole. As a matter of
empirical fact, a man is a valuing creature, and is likely to
remain so. What may happen is that one set of values may get
discarded and another set substituted; for indeed our scales of
values are always changing, sometimes gradually, sometimes
catastrophically. The suggestion that *nothing* matters naturally
arises at times of perplexity like the present, when the claims
upon our concern are so many and conflicting that we might
indeed wish to be delivered from all of them at once. But this
we are unable to do. The suggestion may have one of two
opposite effects, one good and one bad. On the one hand, it
may make us scrutinise more closely values to which we have
given habitual allegiance, and decide whether we really prize
them as much as we have been pretending to ourselves that
we do. On the other, it may make us stop thinking seriously
about our values at all, in the belief that nothing is to be
preferred to anything else. The effect of this is not, as might be
thought, to overthrow our values altogether (that, as I have
said, is impossible); it merely introduces a shallow stagnation
into our thought about values. We content ourselves with the
appreciation of those things, like eating, which most people
can appreciate without effort, and never learn to prize those
things whose true value is apparent only to those who have
fought hard to reach it.

IV

Having made my main point that it is impossible to overthrow
values as a whole, I shall devote the rest of my talk to a discussion of two related topics: the co-called objectivity of values,
and the distinction between subjectivism and relativism. The
first topic may be introduced by considering a possible objection
to my main point. It may be said, All you have done is to show
that people are *in fact* concerned about things. But this established only the existence of values in a *subjective* sense. Now, it

may be said, when people talk about the overthrow of values, they do not mean anything so far-fetched as that people should stop being concerned about things, some about one thing, some about another. But values are overthrown if it is shown, or even if most people think, that these subjective feelings of people are all that there is; that values are not (as I have heard it put) 'built into the fabric of the world'. This objection, then, is a challenge to moral philosophers – which all too many of them have been unwise enough to accept – to demonstrate what is called 'the objectivity of values'.

Now why do I say that it is unwise of moral philosophers to accept this challenge? Because, in the first place, it is always unwise to accept a challenge whose terms you do not understand. And there is one thing that I can say without any hesitation at all – that I do not understand what is *meant* by 'the objectivity of values', and have not met anybody who does. I really think the terms 'objective' and 'subjective' have introduced nothing but confusion into moral philosophy; that they have never been given a clear meaning, and have frustrated all serious discussion of the subject.

For suppose we ask, 'What is the difference between values being objective, and values not being objective?' Can anybody point to any difference? In order to see clearly that there is *no* difference, it is only necessary to consider statements of their position by so-called 'subjectivists'* and 'objectivists' and observe that they are saying the same thing in different words. Let us take as an example *moral* values. An objectivist – for example, an intuitionist – says, 'When I say that a certain act is wrong I am stating the *fact* that the act has a certain non-empirical *quality*, called "wrongness"; and I *discern* that it has this quality by exercising a faculty which I possess called moral intuition'. A subjectivist says, 'When *I* say that a certain act is wrong I am expressing towards it an *attitude* of disapproval which I have'. Now we have all been on many occasions in situations in which we have said, thinking it to be so, that a certain

---

* In this paper (presumably because I thought that it would be more familiar to my listeners) I used the term 'subjectivists' to include emotivists and other non-descriptivists, as well as adherents of the older view referred to at the end of section v, to whom it is more accurately confined. It is very important to distinguish these views (see my article 'Ethics', in *Encyclopedia of Western Philosophy*, ed. Urmson, reprinted in my *Essays on the Moral Concepts*).

act was wrong. This is, as it were, the fixed point in the discussion – the one thing that is clear. We all know how to recognise the activity which I have called 'saying, thinking it to be so, that some act is wrong'. And it is obvious that it is to this activity that the subjectivist and the objectivist are both alluding. This activity which I have called 'thinking something to be wrong' is called by the objectivist 'a moral intuition'. By the subjectivist it is called 'an attitude of disapproval'. But in so far as we can identify anything in our *experience* to which these two people could be alluding by means of these two expressions, it is the same thing – namely the experience which we all have when we think that something is wrong. So far, then, the objectivist and the subjectivist appear to be saying the same thing in different words – words which are distinguished from each other, or from the ordinary way of describing the same experience, only by the degree of abstruseness of their jargon. And things are no better when we come to consider the phrase 'the act has a certain non-empirical quality'. What, I ask, is the difference between the act having this non-empirical quality of wrongness which my intuition discerns, and the act arousing in me an attitude of disapproval? None whatever, as far as I can see.

Though I have no time to pursue this subject, I should like to say in general that for every objectivist way of putting a certain point in moral philosophy, there is always an equivalent subjectivist way, and vice versa. When we see that the quarrels between objectivists and subjectivists are purely verbal, we shall stop wasting our time on them, and devote our attention to more serious problems.

v

At this point the objectivist may protest that there *is* one important – indeed all-important – difference between himself and the subjectivist: namely that according to him (the objectivist) in cases of disagreement about a moral question, or some other question of value, one of the parties to the disagreement must be wrong; and that this, according to the subjectivist, is not so. Suppose that one person (I will call him *A*) says that a certain act is wrong, and another (I will call him *B*) says that it is not wrong. Now the objectivist wants to say two connected things about this situation. The first is that *A* and *B* are *contradicting* one another, and the second is that one of them must be wrong.

Now, when properly understood, these two contentions are both true; but they in no way serve to introduce a distinction between objectivism and subjectivism. For, when properly understood, there is nothing about them which the subjectivist cannot quite happily accept. Let us take first the question of contradiction. It is quite certain – and this the subjectivist would not want to deny – that what *A* says is related to what *B* says in such a way that their two remarks differ in one respect only, that *B*'s remark contains the word 'not' between the words 'is' and 'wrong', whereas *A*'s remark does not. In short, *B* is *negating* what *A* says. Where the objectivist goes wrong is in thinking that this tells us as much as he claims about the logical status of what *A* says. It is just not true that the only statements or other judgements which can be negated are those for which the objectivist would claim objectivity. For example, *commands* can certainly be negated, as when *A* says 'Shut the door' and *B* says 'No, don't'. So the fact that the judgement that a certain act is wrong can be negated does not *even* show that that judgement has not got the same logical status as an imperative; and hence the objectivist is very far from proving that there is an important point of difference here between himself and the subjectivist. Of course a subjectivist can readily admit that moral judgements and other judgements of value can be negated, without committing himself to any particular view about their logical status.

But the objectivist wants to say that the man who says that an act is not wrong is not merely *negating* the judgement that the act is wrong, but *contradicting* it. Does this make a difference? I cannot see that it does. For either the word 'contradict' is being used in such a narrow sense that only those types of judgement which the objectivist calls 'objective' can be said to contradict one another – but in that case the objectivist, in claiming that '*X* is not wrong' contradicts '*X* is wrong', is assuming what he wants to prove; or else it is used in a wide sense, as the equivalent of 'negate'; and in that case the subjectivist can as readily admit that '*X* is not wrong' contradicts '*X* is wrong' as he can admit that they negate one another.

The only dispute so far revealed is a terminological one about the rules which are to govern our use of the word 'contradict'.

In fairness it must be added that an argument of the sort which I have been rebutting can be validly maintained against *certain forms of subjectivism*. Since, however, they are forms which are in any case most implausible, I shall not let them detain us. I mean forms of subjectivism like that which says that '*X* is wrong' means the same as 'I, as a matter of fact, disapprove of *X*'. If this were so, '*X* is wrong' said by *A* would not be contradicted by '*X* is not wrong' said by *B*; but since they do contradict one another, this form of subjectivism has to be rejected. But this argument is so far from refuting the form of subjectivism which I have been discussing (namely that which holds that the man who says '*X* is wrong' is thereby *expressing* disapproval towards *X*) that it does not even serve to make a real distinction between it and objectivism.

VI

What, then, about the other part of the objectivist argument, that which rests upon the fact that if *A* says an act is wrong and *B* says it isn't, one of them must be wrong? Behind this argument lies, I think, the idea that if it is possible to say that it is *right* or *wrong* to say a certain thing, an affinity of some important kind is established between that sort of thing, and other things of which we can also say this. So, for example, if we can say of the answer to a mathematical problem that it is right, and can say the *same thing* of a moral judgement, this is held to show that a moral judgement is in some way *like* the answer to a mathematical problem, and therefore cannot be 'subjective' (whatever that means).

What people who say this sort of thing have not noticed is that the word 'right' is used very generally indeed in our language; it is used for expressing our agreement with almost anything that can be said. Thus, one man may say 'Shut the door' and another may say 'That's right; shut the door'. This in no way establishes that the utterance 'Shut the door' is 'objective'. To say, of something that someone has said, that it is right, is tantamount to repeating it. So if, when someone has said that an act is wrong, I say that he is right to say this, all I am doing is to repeat his judgement in other words; it is as if I were to say 'Yes, it *is* wrong'.*

In the same way, the statement that it is wrong to say that an act is wrong is merely another way of negating or contradicting the statement that the act is wrong. But if so, then what happens to the premisses by which the objectivist sets so much store? We granted him, you remember, that if *A* says that an act is wrong and *B* says it isn't wrong, one of them must be wrong. But this is merely to say that either it is wrong to say that the act is wrong, or it is wrong to say that the act is not wrong. But this reduces, if what I have said is true, to the bare tautology, 'The act is either not wrong or not not wrong', or, cutting out the double negation and reversing the order of terms, 'The act is either wrong or not wrong'. But from this tautology, or from the fact that it is a tautology, nothing whatever follows about the logical status of the judgement that the act is wrong, any more than it did from the fact that *B* was negating what *A* said – at least, *something* may follow about its logical status, but certainly not what the objectivist wants to show. As before, it does not *even* show that moral judgements are different from imperatives. The sentence 'Either shut the door or don't shut the door' expresses a tautology; so, if there is any logical characteristic which is possessed by the judgement that an act is wrong in virtue of its being a tautology that an act is either wrong or not wrong, this same logical characteristic will be possessed by the imperative 'Shut the door'. So it is clear that this argument, too, fails to establish any distinction between the position of the objectivist and that of the subjectivist.

I propose, then, in all seriousness, that the terms 'objective' and 'subjective' be rejected from discussions of moral philo-

---

* This was an oversimplification. To say of something just said that it is right is not equivalent to merely repeating it; and to say that it is wrong is not equivalent to merely uttering its negation. For 'right' and 'wrong' import an element of universalisability which may not have been present in the original utterances. It is implied that to say the same thing in similar circumstances would always be right, or wrong. But since, if the original utterance contained the word 'wrong', this element was already there, no difference is made to the argument. The fact that we can say 'That's right' or 'That's wrong' when someone has uttered an *imperative* suffices to show that the use of those expressions in speaking about moral judgements goes no way at all towards proving that these are factual or 'objective'.

sophy, until someone has succeeded in giving them a use, by pointing to some real distinction which they might be used to draw.

VII

I will conclude this talk by drawing your attention to a common confusion which has, I think, led many people to suppose that there is some vital issue at stake between objectivists and subjectivists. I refer to the confusion between the *ethical* position called 'subjectivism' and the *moral* position called 'relativism'. I think that the confusion between subjectivism and relativism is responsible for a great many of the cross-purposes which are to be found in this part of the subject.

I apologise to those of you who are not familiar with the use of the words 'moral' and 'ethical' to draw the distinction which I wish to draw. If any of you have got used to using the words 'moral' and 'ethical' as if they were synonymous, I hope that you will permit me to explain it, since it is a crucial one.

A moral view is a view about what, in particular or in general, *is* right or wrong, good or bad, etc. An ethical view is a view about the meaning or use of the words or concepts 'right', 'wrong', 'good', 'bad', etc. As Socrates seems to have seen, no progress can be made in moral philosophy before this distinction is grasped. I call relativism a *moral* position, because it is the view that, whatever a person *thinks* is right or wrong, *is* for him right or wrong. Thus, in our example, if *A* thinks that an act is wrong, then for *A* the act is wrong; and if *B* thinks it is not wrong, for *B* it is not wrong. This is indeed an absurd position, at any rate with regard to moral values; it can be shown to lead to contradictions, if the word 'wrong' is being used in its ordinary sense. It would also be, if anybody seriously held it, a very pernicious view, because it might lead its holders to think that serious consideration of moral questions was unnecessary; it would *be* right for them to do whatever they happened to *think* right. I have no time, however, to discuss the truth or falsity of relativism; I only wish to point out that relativism is entirely distinct from subjectivism. Whereas relativism is, as I have said, a view about what, in general, *is* right or wrong, subjectivism is a view about the meaning or use of the words or concepts 'right' and 'wrong'. The first is a moral view, the second an ethical view. You can always tell a moral view from an ethical view, provided that both are carefully expressed, by the following test. In an ethical statement, the words 'right', 'wrong', etc., will always occur in quotation marks. In a moral statement they will occur without quotation marks. Thus the sentence 'It is always right to do what would produce the greatest happiness' expresses a moral view; but the sentence 'The word "right" *means* "productive of the greatest happiness"' expresses an ethical view. The failure to distinguish between these two sorts of view can lead to the greatest confusions – for example, that of thinking that Moore's refutation of naturalism, which could only refute *ethical* theories, disposes of the moral views of Bentham and Mill.

Now subjectivism is a view about the meaning or use of moral or other value-concepts. It is very hard – indeed probably impossible – to state it; for, as I have said, the pair of terms 'objectivism' and 'subjectivism' mark no real distinction. But shall we say that subjectivism is the view that to say 'Such and such an act is right (or wrong)' is to express one's own opinion on a moral question. From this alone it is obvious that, as I have said, there is no real distinction between subjectivism and objectivism; for the objectivist likewise cannot possibly deny that when I say 'Such and such an act is wrong', I am expressing my own opinion. I myself have often been called, by people who don't like what I say, a subjectivist; I should have no objection to this title, if it were not obviously being used as a term of abuse; but it is quite clear to me that the people who use it in this way are certainly confusing subjectivism with relativism, and that they think that I am a relativist; and to such an accusation I should object most strongly.

How often have we not heard people say, 'Unless values are shown to be objective, it will *be* right for everybody to do whatever he *thinks* right'? I hope that by this time I have made clear to you the confusions which lie behind this argument. The first confusion is that of supposing that there is anything to be understood by 'showing values to be objective' (or for that matter 'subjective'). The second is that of thinking that a view, of whatever sort, about the logical nature or status or meaning or use of moral concepts, necessarily commits one to a moral position about what *is* right or wrong; and in particular, to a moral position as patently absurd and pernicious as relativism is.

So, then, what I have to say comes to this. 'The annihilation of values' (if that means 'values as a whole' and not 'some particular set of values') is a pretentious bogey, invented to scare the gullible. For if no sense can be given to questions like 'Are values objective or not?'; 'Are values built into the fabric of the world or not?'; and such like, we do not need to get worried about what is the answer to them. Perhaps I can put it plainly this way. Think of one world into whose fabric values are objectively built; and think of another in which those values have been annihilated. And remember that in both worlds the people in them go on being concerned about the same things – there is no difference in the 'subjective' concern which people have for things, only in their 'objective' value. Now I ask, What is the difference between the states of affairs in these two worlds? Can any other answer be given except 'None whatever'? How, therefore can we torment ourselves with doubts about which of them our own world resembles? My Swiss friend ate a hearty breakfast the next morning; and in this he set us all a good example.

5   Adolescents into Adults

Since I am going to criticise Mr Wilson in some respects, I must start by saying that I am, in all essentials, on the same side as he is. I believe in a distinction between education and indoctrination; and I believe that indoctrination is a bad thing. But I also believe that he stated his case somewhat too extremely; and I think that by so doing he exposed himself to some possible attacks from the propagandists of indoctrination. It is of the highest importance to safeguard Mr Wilson's liberal views against such attacks; for otherwise advocates of the closed mind and the closed society may find it easier to enlist the support of moderates against Mr Wilson; and that would be a pity. I want you to realise, therefore, that my criticisms of Mr Wilson will bulk large in this lecture only because, to avoid repetition, I have left out all those many points on which I should agree with him.

Mr Wilson thinks that education is a good thing, and indoctrination a bad thing; and it is therefore very important for him to state clearly wherein lies the difference. He considers two possibilities: a distinction on the basis of *method*, and a distinction on the basis of *content*. According to the first distinction, education differs from indoctrination because there is a difference in *how* we teach; according to the second, the difference is a difference in *what* we teach. Mr Wilson plumps for the second sort of distinction. He rejects a distinction on the basis of method on the following ground. 'Since young children and infants', he says, 'cannot discuss, the methods we use to educate them are bound to resemble hypnosis and brain-washing

Delivered in 1961 in a series of lectures sponsored by the Manchester University Department of Education, in which I had been preceded by Mr John Wilson, Professor Alasdair MacIntyre, and the Most Revd G. A. Beck. The series was reprinted under the title *Aims in Education*, ed. T. H. B. Hollins (Manchester U.P. 1964).

more than they resemble a democratic exchange of views'
(p. 34). So if indoctrination is a kind of method, we shall have
to admit that this method has a place in the teaching of young
children. But Mr Wilson does not want to admit this, because
he wants to use the word 'indoctrination' for something that is
always bad, on whomsoever it is used. So he cannot admit that
non-rational methods of teaching, such as we have to use
with young children, are indoctrination. So it cannot be the
method that makes a kind of teaching into indoctrination. So,
he thinks, it must be the content – what is taught. We shall
avoid indoctrinating our children if we only educate them
'to adopt behaviour-patterns and to have feelings which are
seen by every sane and sensible person to be agreeable and
necessary. These behaviour-patterns will be rational [he says],
in the sense that they derive from reality rather than from
the values, fears, desires or prejudices of individual people'
(p. 34).

Now this, it seems to me, will not do at all. For who are to
count as sane and sensible people? Most people think that they
themselves and the majority of their friends are sane and sensible
people. So if that is what Mr Wilson says, he will not succeed
in barring the way to a great many educational practices that
I am sure he would want to call indoctrination. Take, for
example, those Roman Catholics who, as the Archbishop of
Liverpool so disarmingly said, 'insist that their children should
be entrusted in school to Catholic teachers [because] the
teacher's causality' – sinister word – 'in the educational process
has results in terms of the appreciation of truth, natural and
supernatural standards of values, moral, aesthetic and literary
which depend ultimately on the personality of the teacher
himself'. These Roman Catholics and the teachers to whom they
entrust their children will no doubt all think that they are sane
and sensible, and that they are in touch with reality (perhaps
they will add, 'natural and supernatural reality'). So when
these children have been duly indoctrinated and turned into
good Roman Catholics, the parents and teachers will claim not
to have offended against Mr Wilson's canon. And the same can
be said if we substitute for 'Roman Catholics', 'Communists',
'Victorians', 'ancient Spartans', 'Trobriand Islanders', or, for
that matter, 'Anglicans'. Yet surely Mr Wilson will want to say,
with Dryden, of such a case:

By education most have been misled;
So they believe, because they were so bred.
The priest continues what the nurse began,
And thus the child imposes on the man.

Dryden, it will be remembered, was speaking of Anglican indoctrination.[1]

If we distinguish indoctrination from education in terms of their content, we are bound to reach this *impasse*. For to make the distinction in this way is to say that there is a *right* content – a *right* doctrine – and, furthermore, that the teacher is the man who knows what it is. It is to say that, provided that this right doctrine is adhered to, it is not indoctrination that is being done, but education. Now I know very well that Mr Wilson does not want to say this, and that it is inconsistent with other things that he says; but I wanted to show just how easily a clever propagandist could twist his words into something that he and any liberal would abhor.

Now why has Mr Wilson fallen into this trap of saying that indoctrination is distinguished from education by its content? I think it is because he does not consider a third possibility, besides saying that the distinction is one of content, and saying that it is one of method. This third possibility is that it is one of *purpose*, or *aim*. This series of lectures is about aims in education, so I am surprised that he did not see this third possibility. Perhaps we can discover why he missed it if we consider in more detail what he said about methods. We have to admit, as he does, that in the early stages of the education of young children, some non-rational methods of teaching, especially in matters of moral behaviour, have to be used. But, he seems to argue, if we have to use these methods, it is pointless to condemn them; but we should be condemning them if we called them 'indoctrination'; therefore we must not call them indoctrination. But since the *methods* do not differ fundamentally from some things that we *should* call indoctrination, the difference between indoctrination and other kinds of teaching cannot be one of method. And with all this I want to agree. If you want to keep 'indoctrination' as a bad word, you cannot start using it of methods which everyone thinks legitimate, because inevitable. But it does not follow that the difference is one of content.

Suppose, for example, that one of my children is going through

[1] *The Hind and the Panther*, III 389.

a phase of telling a lot of lies. It may be that its age is such that no rational discussion of the evil consequences of lying is much good; I may engage in such discussion as a kind of lip-service to my liberal principles, but I may know that what will really influence the child to stop lying is not the discussion, but the tone in which it is conducted. Psychologists can perhaps advise on the best method of getting young children out of the habit of lying; but we can be sure that the method will not be, in Mr Wilson's sense, a rational one. Let us suppose that what happens is that the child senses that I disapprove very strongly of lying, and therefore stops doing it – let us ignore the question of whether this is a psychologically desirable method or not. Have I, by using this non-rational method of affecting the child's behaviour, been *indoctrinating* the child? I do not think so. For I do not *want* the child to remain such that non-rational persuasion or influence is the only kind of moral communication I can have with it. The difference lies in the aim.

There is a German rhyme that I was once taught which goes

> Was der Vater will,
> Was die Mutter spricht,
> Das befolge still.
> Warum? Frage nicht.

> What your father wishes,
> What your mother says,
> Do it in silence.
> Why? Don't ask questions.

Now if I wanted my children to *keep* this sort of attitude to me, or to what I was teaching them, then I should be indoctrinating. But I do not want this. I may have *now* to use non-rational methods of teaching, but my wish is that they may as soon as possible become unnecessary. So, though on occasion I may use the very same methods of teaching as the German who wrote this rhyme, and though my teaching may have exactly the same content, that it is wrong to lie, he is indoctrinating and I am not, because he wants the child always to go on taking its morality from its elders, even after they are dead, whereas I want the child as soon as possible to learn to think morally for itself.

I hope that this example will help you to see what I think is wrong with what some enlightened people say about the moral education of children. One sometimes comes across extreme examples. I know a man who has a child of one year old, and he keeps on saying that he is absolutely determined not to influence his child's moral growth in any way; the child must find its own morality; to try to influence it would be to 'diminish its human personality' as Mr Wilson put it (p. 33); and my friend thinks that there is only a difference in degree between such attempts to influence the morality of one's children and the grossest forms of parental violence.

Now this is obviously absurd, and I do not suggest that Mr Wilson would go as far as this. To begin with, we cannot help influencing our children; the only question is, how, and in what direction. This, I think, Mr Wilson realises. And, if we are going to influence them anyway, what can we do but try to influence them in the best direction we can think of? But indoctrination only begins when we are trying to stop the growth in our children of the capacity to think for themselves about moral questions. If, all the time that we are influencing them, we are saying to ourselves, 'Perhaps in the end they will decide that the best way to live is quite different from what I'm teaching them; and they will have a perfect right to decide that', then we are not to be accused of indoctrinating. We deserve this name only if we say 'I'll try to make this child such a good Communist, or Roman Catholic, or teach him the American way of life so successfully, that he'll never even be able to ask the question whether, or why, one ought to be these things.'

Now what I have said about the *aim* which distinguishes education from indoctrination has a profound bearing upon both the method and the content of education – only these other things are not fundamental; they come from the aim, not it from them. If you are wanting your child in the end to become an adult and think for himself about moral questions, you will try, all the time that you are influencing him by non-rational methods (as you have to), to interest him in rational thinking about morality (this, I know, is a rather solemn expression, but I will try to explain what I mean by it later). That is why I said that I might talk to my child about the evil consequences of lying even though I knew that that was not what would really stop him lying. You can tell what are the aims of a teacher, and whether they are indoctrinatory or not, by studying his methods. Suppose that he carefully arranges for there not to be any free and open discussion of questions of morality until he is absolutely certain that his pupils have, by non-rational methods, been got into a state where they are bound all to give the 'right' answers. Or suppose that he takes enormous care that, though his pupils are encouraged to read books, the books are all ones which say the same thing. Then we shall know what his object is; it is to prevent them asking the questions that might cause them in the end to come to a different moral attitude from himself. Suppose that, on the other hand, he really senses that his pupils are perplexed about some moral question – about sex, for example, or pacifism – and, seeing this, is prepared to discuss it with them, with no holds barred and no questions banned, and is himself prepared to ask the questions again – really ask them – and is prepared to answer them in a different way from the way he has up till now, if that is the way the argument goes. Then we know that he is concerned to get his pupils to think for themselves.

This matter of the teacher himself really treating the questions as open ones is crucial. There is no possibility of pretence here; one cannot act this sort of thing, though we all know parsons and schoolmasters who try. Mr Wilson said something that may mislead when he said that 'questions of moral integrity, honesty, or overt truthfulness do not arise. We live in a mad world; what counts is not preserving our own integrity, but making the world saner' (p. 41). I understood what he meant; he meant that we all sometimes have to temporise with the powers that be. But in our dealings with the young, nothing short of absolute integrity will do. Yet it is not easy really to give one's own deepest moral opinions a turning over. This, however, is what we have to do if we are going to have honest discussions with younger people about the moral problems that perplex them. Because it is a painful process, various ways have been devised of making it less painful. But they are only pretences.

There is the expedient of discussing questions which do not really hurt – academic questions which might have troubled people once but are not the ones that worry us now. There is the even worse expedient of taking questions that really do worry us, but discussing them in a superficial debating style without really becoming involved in them. This is a thing that the young will often do when they have not yet got personally involved in some moral question. It is a thing that they should *never* be encouraged to do, about serious questions.

If a teacher is willing to engage in serious and honest discussion with his pupils about moral questions, to the extent that they are able, then he is not an indoctrinator, even though he may also, because of their age, be using non-rational methods of persuasion. These methods are not, as is commonly supposed, bad in themselves; they are bad only if they are used to produce attitudes that are not open to argument. The fact that a teacher does not himself have such attitudes is the guarantee that he is not an indoctrinator.

I said that the difference in aim between education and indoctrination will result in a difference in content. This is because of the methods which, as we have seen, are appropriate to these two aims. The method appropriate to indoctrination shelters both teacher and pupil from the fresh winds of argument, and this is bound to have the result that things will get taught which would not get taught if the whole process were exposed to these breezes. If the teacher speaks with the voice of authority, however cunningly disguised, and is prepared to use every persuasive device to close the minds of his pupils, there is almost no limit to the irrational taboos and myths that he can successfully inculcate. If, on the other hand, the pupils are not protected against other influences, and the only pressure on them is to consider seriously and rationally what is said and come to their own decisions about it, then it will be less possible to put over these received opinions, and what can be put over will to a certain extent have its content circumscribed. Irrational attitudes cannot flourish when rational methods of argument are seriously practised.

I must say a word here about the attitude a teacher ought to take to the various outside influences, most of them non-rational, which all the time surround his pupils in the press, television, etc. Mr MacIntyre has said something about these; and I do not dissent from the value-judgements he made about the need for encouraging a critical spirit. But why did he have to be so *gloomy*? Knowing him, I was sorry to see him assuming – I hope only temporarily – the mantle of the professional literary pessimist. I was even sorrier to see Mr Wilson, briefly, joining in this familiar chorus; for I myself am much more inclined to sympathise with the attitude of Professor Medawar when he said recently:

> The Predicament of Man is all the rage now that people have sufficient leisure and are sufficiently well fed to contemplate it, and many a tidy little literary reputation has been built on exploiting it; anybody nowadays who dared to suggest that the plight of man might not be wholly desperate would get a sharp rap over the knuckles in any literary weekly (*Mind*, 1961, p. 105).

The state of the world is bad enough in all conscience without adding a dose of quite factitious depression. We might even get so engrossed in moaning about the mess we are in that we became unable to do any constructive thinking about how to improve matters. Indeed, if we do not look out, then Mr MacIntyre will label us 'improvers' (happy term!) if we so much as suggest that there *is* any way in which the world could be made better.

But I hope that teachers, when they rightly take Mr MacIntyre's advice and teach their pupils to criticise what they see around them, will make it clear that 'criticise' is being used in the sense of 'appraise' and not of 'find fault with'. Otherwise they will only be producing a brood of grumblers who have closed their minds to hope. Rather, I would say, teach them to look up out of their books sometimes – even if the books are novels by the most favoured authors; teach them to look out of the window; teach them sometimes, even, to go out of the door – and *look*. If the view that they see is good, or has good in it (as it always will have if they look), teach them to enjoy it, and to help others to enjoy it. If it is bad, or has something bad in it (as it always will), teach them to *think*: What can I do to make it better? How can I get other people to help me make it better – even if people like Mr MacIntyre call us 'improvers' for our pains. This, surely, is better than breaking out into barren and futile jeremiads. But I must not digress.

I was talking about the influences of the press and television. Surely the harm that these do has been somewhat exaggerated, and the good correspondingly underrated. Take advertisements, for example. If all the advertisements were advertising the same brand of soap, as might be the case in a Communist country, then it would be time to get worried – though even in that case good would come of encouraging people to wash. But since they are all advertising different brands, the consumer very soon realises that there is not much difference between the brands, and, though of course he will probably go on buying *some* heavily advertised brand, will not very much care which. The same applies to more important things than soap. Advertisements keep branded goods before our attention; and if this is not done, we shall probably stop buying them and buy some other brand. But in choosing between the brands which are competing in this way, does not the multiplicity of the advertisements make us stop caring which we buy, unless, indeed, we think there is a real difference between the brands? If we do, and if we think it is important to have the best one, do we not then make some effort to find out which the best one is? This, at any rate, is what the schools ought to be teaching their pupils to do; and I do not think it is so difficult. Listen to any two young men discussing the merits of two kinds of motor-car. Which influences them the most – the blurbs in the advertisements or the reports of performance in the technical press, which they read avidly? I must admit that they are also influenced by the appearance of the cars; but ought they not to be? Are we not continually told by the supporters of good industrial design, of whom I am one, to *look* at what we are buying?[1]

The same applies, with very few changes, to politics, morals and religion. If there is plenty of variety in the market place, discernment and discrimination will be fostered. That is one reason why I have the deepest misgivings about what is euphemistically called 'Church Unity'. It is true that all

[1] This lecture was delivered some time before the appearance of the Pilkington Report. I do not wish these remarks to be taken as supporting the opponents of the report. The danger of commercial television is not that it provides a large quantity of popular entertainment – any medium which serves a mass audience is bound to do this. The danger is rather that if commercial advantage only is followed, this kind of programme will push out everything else, or almost so. What is needed in broadcasting and television is not to reduce the quantity of low-brow programmes but to improve their quality, and at the same time to provide an ample and varied supply of programmes for educated people. If this is done, and if schoolmasters do their job, I am optimistic enough to predict that an ever-growing audience will listen to or watch them. But I think that this is more likely to happen if the public-service side of television is strengthened in the way the Report recommends.

Christians ought to be able to worship at the same table, and to live and pray together without acrimony. And I am convinced that nothing now prevents them doing this but the purely political rivalries between the various ecclesiastical machines. But in order to bring about unity of worship, is it necessary to have a single 'Church' in the organisational sense? It seems to me that to do this would be to create a religious monopoly of the most pernicious kind, a sort of totalitarian Church, whose main function would be to perpetuate the power of its leaders to indoctrinate and thereby control. So I hope that you will not misunderstand me when I say that more good than harm comes from competition, both in commerce and in politics and in religion.

So, by and large, I think that schoolmasters have little to fear from the press and television, provided that there is diversity, and provided that the schoolmasters are themselves trying to educate and not to indoctrinate. Nor, I should like to add, subject to the same proviso, have they anything to fear from philosophers. You may have noticed, as I did, a rather sinister letter which appeared in *The Times* recently. A correspondent, writing about a project to build a Roman Catholic hostel in Oxford, which had been condemned by the Roman Catholic chaplaincy as a breach of a gentleman's agreement to abstain from proselytising, complained that the really bad proselytising in Oxford was done on behalf of atheists by some people he called 'analytical philosophers', who had, he said, destroyed the faith of three young Anglican friends of his. He seemed unaware that the group of philosophers whom he calls 'analytical' contains several devout Roman Catholics, as well as some devout Anglicans. What had happened to his friends was, I am sure, something like this: before they came to Oxford, they had been indoctrinated by their parents or schoolmasters with some spurious arguments for religion; when they got to the university and came to see that the arguments were bogus, they reacted, perhaps temporarily, in the opposite direction. But this is the fault of people who think that they are doing a service to religion by this kind of indoctrination. I never do anything of this kind, but practise 'analytical philosophy' according to my ability; yet about one of my pupils in every twelve has become a parson.

There was one more gap in Mr Wilson's exposition that I should like to fill, if I can. Having distinguished between education and indoctrination in terms of their contents, it was important for him to state clearly the distinction between the contents of these two things. This he did not do, though he gave examples; and I have already said that it is no use saying that we can avoid indoctrination if we teach only those moral opinions that sane and sensible people would agree with – for who are the sane and sensible people? Now I have maintained, for this very reason, that a distinction in terms of content will not do; but that if we have the aim of educating people, this aim will determine the method, and the method will to a certain extent determine the content. But this is not nearly specific enough; I am sure that you will want to ask me what, in more detail, *is* this method of rational discussion that I have been advocating, and why I think that it will be inimical to what I have called myths and taboos and will let in only rational opinions.

Now to ask this is to ask me to launch out into a treatise on moral philosophy. I could not possibly say anything at all profound in the time remaining.[1] But I will try to give you an outline of what I think. The two essential features of moral opinions are, first, that they are not about matters of fact but about how one ought to behave (this is what is meant by calling moral judgements 'prescriptive'); and secondly, that if I hold a certain moral opinion about an act done by one person, I must hold the same moral opinion about a similar act done by a similar person in similar circumstances. This is often referred to by moral philosophers as the principle of the 'universalisability' of moral judgements. Both of these are *logical* features of moral judgements; if we do not understand either of them, we do not understand the uses of the moral words. Roughly speaking, a moral opinion is *rational* if it is not taken on authority as a matter of fact but freely accepted as a prescription for living, and if it is recognised as holding good irrespective of whether it is I that am the subject of it or someone else. The reason why, if someone transgresses either of these two requirements, he is not being rational, is that they are requirements of logic, having their basis in the meanings of the moral words; therefore someone who transgresses them is being as illogical as someone who says, 'All the books are red but there is one which is not'.

---

[1] I have said what I can on this subject in my book, *Freedom and Reason* (Oxford, 1963).

Now the consequences of the first of these features of moral judgements for moral discussion have been adequately dealt with by Mr Wilson. Briefly, since moral judgements are not statements of fact or pieces of information, they cannot be taught out of a textbook like the names of the capitals of European countries. It is not a question of *informing* those whom we are teaching, but of their coming to accept a certain opinion for their own.

But Mr Wilson did not, so far as I can remember, say anything about the second feature. Now, as I could show if I had time, it is this feature, in conjunction with the first, which really limits the moral opinions that we can hold. It is by applying these two characteristics of moral judgements together that argument really gets a grip on moral questions. What we have to teach people, if we are educating them morally, is to ask themselves the question, 'What kind of behaviour am I ready to prescribe for myself, given that in prescribing it for myself, I am prescribing it also for anybody in a like situation?' I could, but I will not, go on to show how this question, if we can get people to ask it, circumscribes their moral choices in a rational way, so that the abandonment of taboos and irrational prejudices which Mr Wilson recommends does not, as has sometimes been feared, open the way to unbridled licence.

I said, 'If we can get people to ask it'. But one of the most important things for educators to remember is that morality, as governed by this question, is a very *difficult* thing to accept. Because it is a difficult and sophisticated thing, it does not come naturally to children. It is no use, as Mr Wilson sometimes seems to imply, merely leaving children as free as possible from external moral influences, and hoping that the thing will just grow. It *will* grow in most cases, but only because the seed is there in our own way of thinking, from which it is well-nigh impossible to isolate a child. It is not, however, something innate; it is a question of tradition; morality is something that has to be handed down; if it were not – if the process were interrupted – our children really would grow up as barbarians.

What has to be passed on is not any *specific* moral principle, but an understanding of what morality is and a readiness to think in a moral way and act accordingly. This could be put in other words by saying that children have to learn to use the moral words such as 'right' and 'wrong' and to understand their meaning. That is why it is so very important for philosophers to study what their meaning is – how silly it is to say that philosophers ought not to occupy themselves with matters of words! It must be emphasised that it is not the content of any particular morality that is being handed down – that would be indoctrination, if the aim was, at all costs, to implant *these* particular moral principles. It is not a particular morality, but morality itself that we are teaching; not to think this or that (because we say so or because the good and great have said so) but to think morally for oneself. And to learn this is to learn how to *speak* morally, understanding what one says.

Doubtless it is not possible in practice to pass on the mere form of morality without embodying it in some content; we cannot teach children the abstract idea of a moral principle as such without teaching them some concrete moral principles. And naturally we shall choose for this purpose those principles which we think in themselves desirable. This, as I said, is not indoctrination provided that our aim is that the children should in the end come to appraise these principles for themselves. Just so, one cannot teach the scientific outlook without teaching some science; but the science that is taught could be radically altered in the light of later researches, and yet the scientific outlook remain. The good science teacher will teach what he thinks to be the truth, but his teaching will not have proved vain if what has been taught is later rejected as false; and similarly, if we can teach children what morality is, using our own moral thinking as an example, we shall have done our job, even if the moral thinking which they later do leads them to different conclusions.

Fortunately there is a close connexion between the form of morality and its content. As I could show if there were time, and have attempted to show in my book which I have already referred to, once the form of morality is accepted in our thinking, it quite narrowly circumscribes the substance of the moral principles that we shall adopt. We can therefore happily start by securing the adherence of our children – if necessary by non-rational methods – to the moral principles which we think best, provided that these are consistent with the form of morality; but we must leave them at liberty later to think out for themselves different principles, subject to the same proviso.

Now in conveying to children what morality is, our method

is governed by what it is that we are trying to convey. Because moral judgements are things that one has to make for oneself, we have to get children to understand, in the end, that 'wrong' does *not* mean 'what the parent or the schoolmaster forbids'; the schoolmaster might forbid it, and the child might still think it right, and the child might have a right to its opinion. On this aspect of the matter Mr Wilson has laid enough stress.

But secondly, and arising out of the universalisability of moral judgements, the child has got to realise, somehow, that what is wrong for another to do to him is wrong for him to do to another. This is the foundation of all that part of morality which concerns our dealings with other people. And this gives us an important clue about method. Children must learn to think about what it is like to be the other person. They must cultivate their sympathetic imaginations. And this is not easy. It will not be brought about without effort on the part of parents and schoolmasters. And it will not be brought about by rational discussion alone. Suppose that somebody who took Mr Wilson too literally, and did not realise the importance of this feature of morality which he left out, went away from his lecture determined to confine himself, in his dealings with the young, in the early stages to plain imperatives like 'Go to bed', which make no pretence to be moral and therefore can do no harm, and in the later stages to rational discussion. His charges really would, if he could observe this principle in isolation from other influences, grow up without an understanding of morality.

Of course, this is unlikely to happen in practice, because there are, fortunately, other influences on children than their parents and schoolmasters, and many of them are media for the handing on of an understanding of moral thinking. The mere use of moral words by a child's contemporaries does a great deal. So nobody is going to be able to carry out this too literal interpretation of Mr Wilson's prescription; and we are in no real danger of relapsing into a Hobbesian state of nature, in which every man's hand is against every man. But unless *some* non-rational methods are used, it is unlikely that all our children will come to absorb this principle as deeply as we could wish; and to that extent less of their thinking about action will be moral thinking, and their actions will show this.

The non-rational influences I have in mind are chiefly two: environment and example. The examples that one has set before one are *part* of one's environment, so this division is not a neat one; but it will do for what I want to say. The first important thing, if we want our children to learn morality, is that they should be put into an environment in which the unpleasant effects of other people's lapses on them are as obvious as possible. This means that they must have plenty of opportunity of rubbing up against other people in some sort of more or less constant group – more or less constant, because they have to have time to get to think of the other people in the group as people (i.e. as like themselves), or the treatment will not work. In such an environment, children can easily absorb the lesson that they ought to do unto others as they would that others should do unto them. The family is such a group; but families are not enough, because some families fall down on the job, and delinquency is sometimes the result. Schools, therefore, have a lot to contribute, as have clubs; and they have one very important advantage over the family, that in them the child rubs up against a large number of people of his own age, whom, therefore, it is easy for him to think of as like himself, sharing his likes and dislikes, and therefore hurt by the things that hurt him and pleased by the things that please him. It will be easier in such a group for the child to learn to universalise his moral judgements.

Secondly, the group must have a good tradition. If it is a St Trinian's, the child will indeed suffer from the misdeeds of other children, but its reaction will be one of self-defence merely, and we shall have a reign of blackboard jungle law. There has to be a tradition of kindness to, and co-operation with, other people. I am sorry to repeat these platitudes; but I want to show you how they are the consequences of the nature of morality; *that* they are true is obvious, but we need to understand *why* they are true.

But, thirdly, how do we start these good traditions? This seems to me to be the most important, perhaps the only essential, function of the adult in moral education. After a certain age, children and young people will get their moral ideas and ideals and attitudes for the most part from each other; either from their schoolfellows or from the rest of the gang. So the most important point at which the adult can intervene, *if* he can intervene, is by influencing the morality of the group; and this is done by example.

Now I do not want you to make at this point what I think is a very easy mistake to make. 'Setting a good example' by itself is no use at all. The people to whom it is being set must want to follow it. We need to know what can make them want to follow it. I think that all good schoolmasters know the answer to this question. Children desire to imitate particular traits of a person whom they desire to imitate as a whole. If an adult is *merely* an example of desirable moral attitudes, they will not take much notice. But if there are a great many other things about him that they admire – usually things that have nothing to do with morals – then they will swallow the moral attitudes too.

There are a lot of things that children and young men will willingly learn from their elders. Sometimes, if they are intellectually gifted, they will even willingly learn from them Latin and French; but this is unfortunately not common. They will, however, very frequently be anxious to learn to play football, or sail boats, or play the violin in the orchestra; and if there is an adult whom they trust to teach them these things, they will pick up from him much besides. That is why those who are employing schoolmasters look, not merely for good teachers of Latin or French or football or music – they look for men who, in teaching these things, will hand on something that is of much more importance.

This is one of the sources of the value of so-called out-of-school activities like games and music, as well as the more wide-ranging ones like sailing and mountaineering, which are now becoming so popular. They are vehicles for the transmission of an understanding of morality from one generation to another. But they also have another importance from the moral point of view: all of them, to a greater or less extent, are co-operative activities; they therefore require, in all who participate in them, a standard of behaviour. On a small scale, but intensely, they reproduce those very factors which, I suppose, have led to the development of morality in civilised communities at large. One learns, in such teams or groups, to submit oneself to a rule – a rule not dictated by some particular person, but freely accepted by all the participants, either because, like the rule about not passing forward, or like watching the conductor, it is a necessary condition for the doing of *this* particular activity called orchestral playing or rugger; or else because it is dictated by the realities of the situation, like not sailing by the lee, or not getting lost in the mountains and causing other people to organise search parties to rescue you. The second of these two kinds of rules is the more important; and therefore I think that the second of the two kinds of activity – that which includes sailing and fell walking – deserves the increasing attention that it is getting from schoolmasters. Perhaps music should be after all included with these; for music also is in touch with reality; if you play a wrong note it is not just that you have broken the rule of a game. But games, in the narrow sense, will always have a certain artificiality. And of course compulsory games, whose rules are not freely accepted by the participants, do no good at all from the point of view that we are considering, though they may have some of the other virtues that used to be claimed for them.

The point that I wish to emphasise by saying these familiar things is that these practices, which schoolmasters have found useful, owe their usefulness to the nature of what they are trying to hand on, namely morality. Morality has, of its nature, to be freely accepted; therefore in this respect the rules of sea-manship are a better analogue of it – and their strict observance actually a better example of it – than the rules in the school rule-book. And secondly, morality is impartial as between persons; therefore, to learn to accept rules applicable impartially within a group is a good schooling in morality. There is, of course, a danger in this; we all know the kind of team spirit which counts anything as fair against the other side, or against those outside the team. To become a loyal member of a group is an important step on the way from egoism to altruism; but it is a step at which it is all too easy to get stuck.

I must add here that, important as membership of groups is in the formation of moral ideas, it is important also for the development of the individual's personality that he should be able sometimes to break away from the group and pursue his own ideals, if necessary entirely by himself, if he is that sort of person. For all morality is not social morality – to think that it is, is a mistake that has often been made by moral philosophers and by educationists. There are moral ideals, some of them very fine ones, which have nothing to do with our fellow men; and although it is necessary to learn to live with our fellow men, it is restricting to the personality to be unable to get away from them. This educational requirement has, like the others, a theoretical basis in moral philosophy; but for reasons of time I shall not be able to tell you what it is.

I have mentioned two ways in which adults can help to pass on the idea of morality to another generation. But the power of adults to do this is severely limited by what adolescents will accept from adults. They want to imitate adults; but they want to imitate them in one thing above all – *in being adult*. They want, that is to say, to be their own masters. They will only feel that they have really succeeded in imitating the adult when they have got the adult out of the way.

This lends peculiar interest to an experiment which you may have seen described in *The Times* recently.[1] At Crawley, the local authority, having available some Nissen huts in a clearing in some woods near the town, turned them over without supervision to various youth organisations to use for a variety of purposes ranging from, I think, boxing to making model aeroplanes. The huts were intensively used, and looked after with very little damage, and obviously filled a need which must exist in other places than Crawley. When I say 'without supervision', this is not strictly accurate; there is a forest warden of the Forestry Commission who lives on the spot and keeps a fatherly eye on the buildings. But the point is that all the organisation is done by the groups themselves without any adult interference. The success of this experiment should not make us ask, as apparently some people have asked, 'Are youth leaders (or for that matter schoolmasters) really necessary?' For of course good youth leaders and good schoolmasters will always be in short supply; what we learn from this experiment is one way of making the supply go further. Sometimes the best way adults can help adolescents to grow up is by keeping in the background; and of course this lesson has an application in schools too, and still more in universities.

It is by this readiness to retire gracefully, indeed, that we can most easily tell the educator from the indoctrinator. I said earlier that I agreed with Mr Wilson that education might sometimes have to use the same methods as indoctrination, and that therefore the two cannot be distinguished by their methods. I said that they were distinguished by their aims; the educator

[1] *The Times*, 18 Feb 1961, p. 9.

is trying to turn children into adults; the indoctrinator is trying to make them into perpetual children. But I said that the aim would all the same make a difference to the method; and this becomes evident, if we watch the process over a period. Many of the methods I have alluded to can be used for indoctrination in the most deplorable doctrines; the Nazi youth organisations used them, fortunately without lasting success, to pervert a whole generation of German youth while they thought they were just youth-hostelling or playing games or whatever it might be. But if one watches carefully one will notice a difference. The educator is waiting and hoping all the time for those whom he is educating to start *thinking*; and none of the thoughts that may occur to them are labelled 'dangerous' *a priori*. The indoctrinator, on the other hand, is watching for signs of trouble, and ready to intervene to suppress it when it appears, however oblique and smooth his methods may be. The difference between these two is like the difference between the colonial administrator who knows, and is pleased, that he is working himself out of a job, and the one who is determined that the job shall still be there even when he himself retires.

So there is, in the end, a very great difference between the two methods. At the end of it all, the educator will insensibly stop being an educator, and find that he is talking to an equal, to an educated man like himself – a man who may disagree with everything he has ever said; and, unlike the indoctrinator, he will be pleased. So, when this happens, you can tell from the expression on his face which he is.

6 What is Life?

Life presents us with many problems; but is 'What is Life?' one of them? Don't we all know what life is? Or do we? Surgeons have recently learnt how, in certain cases, to start a man's heart working after it has stopped; this has long been possible with the breathing, which was once thought to be a criterion of life – 'If that her breath will mist or stain the stone, why then she lives', says King Lear. What then is the state of the man who has stopped breathing, and whose heart has stopped beating, but who is subsequently resuscitated? Is he alive or dead? If we say he is alive, why do we not apply the same term to another man, in a precisely similar condition, who does not happen to be lucky enough to have his seizure when there is a surgeon at hand, and who is therefore not resuscitated? How would we *date* the death of the second man? If we say that his life ended when he had the seizure, we ought in consistency to say that the first man, too, died when he had the seizure, and was subsequently brought back to life. But then is death not 'the undiscover'd country from whose bourn no traveller returns'? We feel an aversion to saying that a man has been dead, if he subsequently 'comes to life again'.

What, again, are we to say about the lady in Montreal who recently stopped breathing after having been in a coma since a traffic accident twelve years previously? Suppose that during these twelve years we knew for certain that she could never recover consciousness. In that case, some would claim that her life ended at the time of the accident, and that her subsequent state was one of, at the most, 'arrested death'. Patients whose brain has been injured by accident or disease are nowadays kept breathing for long periods in respirators without the hope of ever regaining consciousness.

Suppose that some person had administered poison to the

This is the English version, published in *Crucible* (1965), of an article commissioned by *Elseviers Weekblad* (1964).

Montreal patient between the time of the accident and the time when she stopped breathing twelve years later. Would he have been guilty of murder? Or suppose that a man's heart has stopped beating, but could be restarted; and that, before this is done, somebody shoots him through the head. If the man is no longer alive, then the man who shoots him can hardly be said to be guilty of murder; for you cannot murder a man without killing him, and you cannot kill a man who is not alive. Yet we feel that some sort of crime has been committed more serious than that of mutilating a corpse.

Here is another very similar problem, which is important for the same sort of reasons. A child is born deformed. Is it a man? On what does the answer to this question depend? Suppose that the child has only rudimentary limbs; does that entitle me to say that it is not human? Or suppose that it appears physically normal, but turns out to have the mind of an animal. Suppose, even, to take a fantastic extreme case, that what is born is a perfectly formed puppy. Perhaps nobody would say, in the last-mentioned case, that a man who took the life of the puppy would be guilty of murder. In the recent tragic series of deformed births due to thalidomide, there were those who held that extreme deformity entitled us to say that a child was not human, and therefore that to take its life would not be murder. Most of us shrank from this conclusion. What seemed to be needed was a definition of 'human'; the question 'What is Man?', like the question 'What is Life?', began to look like a crucial, and at the same time an insoluble, question.

So let us ask, more fundamentally, what it is about our thinking that has got us into trouble. The fault lies in our unreasonable wish to have simple rules for our conduct in a complex world. We are on a wild-goose-chase if we are looking for a set of a few simple rules, without exceptions, which will give us the right answer to all moral problems. Life is too complicated for that. There is no substitute for careful thought about particular cases. The Israelites, who started with the Ten Commandments, ended up with the books of Leviticus, Numbers and Deuteronomy.

If we are seeking a simple rule, the command 'Thou shalt do no murder' looks like a strong candidate. It has not got quite the simplicity of 'Thou shalt not kill'; but the latter has seemed obviously *too* simple to most people except the followers of

Tolstoy and some Oriental sects. 'Thou shalt do no murder' looks at first sight more promising. It allows us to kill the people that most of us think it is all right to kill, and forbids us to kill anybody else. The concept 'murder' is, indeed, tailored to do just this. At the moment most people think it is not murder to kill one's country's enemies in battle. But if we all became pacifists, and thought that it was wrong to kill people even in battle, we might start calling it murder to do so. The word 'murder' scarcely serves to identify the cases in which it is wrong to kill; all it does is to docket or catalogue the most important class of them in a conveniently simple way – provided that we are dealing only with ordinary cases and not with the queer cases mentioned earlier. When we come to them, we have to think again. Even in the case of killing in battle, which is familiar enough, try settling the question of whether it is wrong by asking the question whether it is murder. We at once realise that we cannot know whether it is murder until we have already decided whether it is wrong.

So, when we consider whether it is all right to kill a child without arms and legs, or one even more seriously deformed, or whether it is wrong to stop feeding artificially a patient who will remain unconscious until he ceases to breathe years later, the word 'murder' is not going to help us. We have to consider the case before us. If it were analogous in all respects to more normal cases, then we should not be in the quandary we are in. If, instead of considering the peculiarities of the particular case, we confuse ourselves by trying to force it into ready-made categories like 'murder', 'alive', 'human', etc., which were not designed to deal with it, we shall go on being puzzled – go on asking the apparently insoluble questions 'What is Murder?', 'What is Life?', 'What is Man?' But the moral question we are asking cannot really depend on definitions of words. If what we want are definitions of words, we can have plenty. There are any number of ways in which 'life' might be defined. Each defines a slightly different concept. Different people, for different purposes (of medical or legal practice, or biological research, or theological or moral discussion) will choose different definitions. None of these gives *the* meaning of the word 'life'. The people we have described are alive in some senses, in others not. Provided we keep these senses distinct, and thus are clear about the facts of a situation, there may be some hope of arriving at an answer to the moral question that will satisfy us.

This advice will cause some people to despair. They will say, 'We have learnt from our parents and priests the simple rule "Thou shalt do no murder"; if you take this away from us, how shall we ever know that it is wrong to kill anybody? You tell us to consider particular cases; but how are we supposed to do this?' The answer to this is a Socratic one: 'You do not know that it is wrong to kill anybody; you have only taken it on trust from your parents and priests. If you wish to understand how to decide what it is right to do in the queer cases, you will have to think hard about why it is right to do what most of us do in the ordinary cases.' And that is how moral philosophy begins. But it is not likely to produce any simple labour-saving rules; for life is not like that.

7   Peace

I am going to talk, in a philosophical way, about the attitudes
which have to be adopted if there is to be any hope of world
peace; and it is a great pleasure to be giving this talk in the
Australian National University, where, perhaps, these attitudes
are to be found, if not universally, at least more frequently than
almost anywhere else in the world. I am not going to try to give
a general answer to the question of how to preserve peace. This
is a question to which experts of all kinds have devoted their
attention – experts in strategy, diplomacy, political theory, even
sociology, psychology, ethology and medicine. Although Kant
once wrote a book on the subject, philosophers have, as such,
no specialised knowledge of any of the fields which are generally
thought to be relevant to the question today. If one wanted,
for example, to know where the balance of military power lay,
and how it would alter under certain conditions, one would be
wise to ask a strategical expert and not a philosopher. It may
therefore seem to you surprising that I, a philosopher, should
have chosen to speak on this subject; you may wonder what I
have, professionally, to contribute.

The nature of the philosopher's contribution and interest
will become clear if we consider what are the two main forces
in the world which endanger peace. Both these forces are *ideas*;
unless men were in the grip of these ideas, they would not start
wars, whatever the military or the diplomatic situation – indeed,
if the ideas which governed men's actions were different, the
military and diplomatic situation would also be different. I shall
call these two ideas *nationalism* and *fanaticism*. We cannot hope
to come to grips with these forces unless we first understand
them; and it is this kind of understanding of ideas that the
philosopher seeks. He cannot make people think one thing or

The sixth annual lecture of the Research Students' Association, Australian
National University, delivered at Canberra in 1966.

another; but he can make people understand better what they are thinking – and when they understand this, they may come to think something different.

Nationalism and fanaticism are not the monopoly of any particular party or ideology. Fascists of the old kind can of course be both nationalists and fanatics; but so can communists. We all know that Hitler was both a nationalist and a fanatic; but the same is true of the Chinese leaders today, and of Senator Goldwater. The ideas which I am going to discuss, and which I say are the main causes of war, operate at a much deeper level than these so-called ideological divisions.

What a man does, whether in politics or out of it, will in the main depend on what he thinks right. He may, of course, be deflected by physical or moral weakness; but we can perhaps ignore this, because a man who (these days) can achieve for himself a position of power in which his decisions profoundly affect the course of history, is likely to be deflected by weakness less than other men. In the main, such people do pursue single-mindedly what they think to be right. Hitler, for example, was not a weak man; he did to the utmost of his power what he thought to be right – and we could say the same of many other people who have influenced history, even if we find it hard to understand how they can have thought that they were doing right. Here, indeed, lies our problem; for if we could understand the thinking processes which could persuade a man like Hitler that what he was doing was right, we might be on the way to immunising people against such ideas. Is it perhaps true that, if philosophers had done their job better in the last two centuries (both the job of clarifying ideas to themselves, and the job of getting other people to understand them) there would not have been a Nazi movement?

The key to this understanding lies in the word 'right' itself. Philosophers have often been attacked (as indeed Socrates was) for wasting their time on questions about words. In earlier times the attack was usually directed against what was called 'metaphysics'; and indeed even now we often hear a contrast made between the making of subtle and useless metaphysical distinctions and the more down-to-earth study of practical questions. Nowadays, in the English-speaking world, what is attacked is usually called 'linguistic philosophy'. But both attacks have really the same target, namely philosophy itself. For philosophy, which seeks the understanding of ideas, cannot achieve it by any other means than by understanding the words in which these ideas are expressed. When people attack it, it is often because, although they would never acknowledge this, they prefer not to understand clearly what they are saying.

To illustrate this, let us take this word 'right'. I must first clear away a difficulty which is bound to trouble us unless I deal with it (albeit very summarily) now. I said that Hitler did what he thought to be right. And I would say the same of some other lesser nationalists, such as Mussolini, Sukarno and de Gaulle. You may say, 'Surely Hitler knew very well that what he was doing was wrong; but he did it all the same. It was not, admittedly, weakness of will that made Hitler do what he did; but he did it, knowing it to be wrong, just because he was a wicked man.'

I am sure that we shall get nowhere with understanding either Hitler or a great many other delinquents if we say this sort of thing. In England it has recently become a popular sport with some young people to put slabs of concrete on railway lines, or unscrew the rails in the middle of tunnels, just for the hell of it. Only, I think, one engine-driver has been killed so far. They caught a boy doing this, and the magistrate asked him in court whether he did not think it was wrong to do something which could endanger the lives of hundreds of people. He answered, 'No, I didn't think it wrong'. Hitler would have given the same answer.

Admittedly, there is a sense of 'right' in which Hitler would have agreed that what he was doing was not right. That is to say, he would have admitted that what he was doing was contrary to the moral convictions of most 'civilised' men (a class whom he despised). But, nevertheless, he thought that he had a higher destiny and that he ought to fulfil it – that he would have been doing wrong if he had shirked it. And the boys who sabotage the railways think they are doing right. Imagine the feelings of such a boy if you suggested to him, while he was on the way to join the gang, that he would do better to go home to bed. Would he not reply that that would be letting the others down? If, out of weakness, he succumbed to the suggestion, would he not experience remorse? Hitler, no doubt, experienced remorse if ever, in a moment of weakness, he failed to live up to his destiny.

So, to understand these in other ways very different people, we have to understand the processes of thought which can lead them to think that what they are doing is right. We shall completely fail to grasp the situation, and all our remedies will be practically ineffective, if we start from the assumption that their actions are obviously wrong, and that they know it as well as we do. I do not think, indeed, that the proposition that their actions are right will be sustained, in the face of clear thinking, by anybody who is not psychologically disturbed. But if we start from the realisation that they do think this, then there is some hope; for if we can remedy the causes of the psychological imbalance, and get people like, for example, those who gave Hitler such massive support, to think clearly, then they may stop thinking it right to do these terrible things. And the philosopher has a contribution to make to achieving this – though only one contribution among many that are needed.

So let us try to understand this word 'right' better, in the sense in which Hitler thought he was doing right. If we do understand it properly, we know that you cannot, without logical inconsistency, say that some action is right, while at the same time maintaining that some other precisely similar action is not right. Two actions cannot differ *only* in that one is right and the other not. There must be some other difference. This logical feature of the word 'right' is the basis of nearly all moral arguments; and the philosopher who has laid most stress on it is Kant. In order to see the force of this logical point in arguments about war, it is absolutely crucial to distinguish between what I am calling nationalism and what I am calling fanaticism. I am going to start with nationalism; then, when we have understood that, I shall go on to point out the differences between it and fanaticism.

A nationalist is a person who thinks it right to pursue, single-mindedly, the interests of his own nation, to the disregard of those of other nations. If anybody tries to advocate nationalism in a pure and undisguised form, the feature of the word 'right' that I have just mentioned provides us with a powerful argument against him. Will you allow me to illustrate this by means of a very simple imaginary example? Although imaginary, it brings out the essential features of the argument, which a more complicated and true-to-life example might obscure. We can add the complications later.

Imagine that there are two islands in the Pacific, identical in shape and other geographical features (for example, suppose that they consist of flat circular atolls of identical size with lagoons in the middle). And suppose that these islands are inhabited by two tribes whose racial characteristics, customs, language, etc., are precisely similar; and that these tribes spend their whole time making war on each other. Let us call the two islands Alpha and Beta. Now suppose that we say to some patriotic Alphan: 'You think it right for yourself and your fellow countrymen to go and scalp the Betans and rape their wives; what do you think about the Betans coming and doing the same to you?' He cannot, if he understands the word 'right', answer that what is right for the Alphans is wrong for the Betans; for in our artificial example we have postulated that there is no difference between the two islands or the two tribes. There can therefore be nothing to make any act right in one case but wrong in the other.

On the other hand, he is not likely to say that, just as it is right for him to scalp the Betans if he can, so it is right for them to scalp him if they can. It is probable, rather, that the concept 'right' would not come into use under conditions such as I have described; if it did come into use, the effect might be to make them stop scalping each other – never underestimate the power of a concept!

But in fact it is unlikely that the simple state of affairs that I have described could ever occur in real life. There would always be differences between the two islands and their inhabitants; and it would be open to our patriotic Alphan to say that some of these differences were morally relevant. They might be natural differences (for example, the Betans might have darker skins or hooked noses); or they might be cultural differences (they might have a totem pole with a different bird on top; or they might wear beads of a different colour in their necklaces). The chief value of such differences in national customs and national uniforms is that they make it possible, even when there are not enough natural differences between tribes, for the nationalist to escape from the argument which we have just brought against him. Our Alphan can say, 'It is right for people who customarily wear red beads to slaughter people who customarily wear blue beads; but it is wrong for the blue-beaders to slaughter the red-beaders.' There is nothing in such an argument to offend against *logic*; and indeed such manoeuvres have been the stock-in-trade of nationalists from the most primitive times to the present day. How else are we to explain the popularity of national uniforms and tribal customs? They enable us to maintain the differences between nations which are otherwise very similar, so that patriotic people can justify to themselves actions towards members of other nations which they would think it the greatest of wickedness to do to members of their own nation. If a member of another nation wears strange clothes, or eats garlic, or still more if he is black, or circumcised, doesn't it seem much easier to turn a machine-gun on him? Or if he talks an unintelligible language or says the Lord's Prayer without the doxology, or the Creed with an iota added in the wrong place, or in Latin, can't we understand people finding it easy to think that he ought to be extirpated? The religious and other wars that have ravaged Europe and the rest of the world throughout recorded history will provide many examples of cases in which groups of people fought one another basically just because they were different groups of people and the members of each were seeking their own group's advantage, but in which, nevertheless, the differences (often what seem to us trivial differences) between the groups served to justify and thus preserve the hostile attitudes which alone make war tolerable. If you want to feel happy about fighting somebody, you have to think of him as an *alien*, whether in terms of nation, or race, or class, or creed.

Is there any argument which will prevail against a nationalist who insists that differences like those I have mentioned are morally relevant – that they justify him in treating differently people so differentiated? As we shall see, there is no ineluctable argument; there is only what we may call a test of sincerity – a test which the nationalist can only pass if he turns his national-ism into something else, namely fanaticism. If he remains a pure nationalist, and will not take this step, his position is untenable. Suppose that we ask our Alphan to, as we say, put himself in the place of someone, say a Betan, who has a different skin-colour or different tribal customs from his own. He has to consider a case in which *he* has a black skin, or has been brought up to wear blue beads. Does he think that it would be right, then, for people to scalp *him*? Here we are asking him to consider a purely hypothetical proposition; but if he considers it in earnest – and it is a necessary part of moral thought to be willing to do this – he will surely answer that he does not think it would be right for people to scalp him. But if so, then for the logical reasons which I have already mentioned, he cannot say, as he was saying, that it is right for people with white skins and wearing red beads to scalp people with black skins wearing blue beads.

The readiness to consider such hypothetical cases is, as I said, a necessary part of moral thought. A man may, of course, refuse to consider them. It was reported at the trial of Eichmann, who was the chief executive in the Nazi programme for exterminating the Jews, that once a colleague said to him: 'God forbid that any nation should treat us Germans as we are treating the Jews!' Eichmann's reply was, 'Don't be sentimental; it's an order of the Führer'. I am not saying that, if people close their minds in this way, a philosopher can open them again. But if people are prepared to think, a philosopher may bring out the implications of what they are thinking; and then they may stop thinking it.

I hope you will notice that it makes no difference to this argument if the Alphan, or if Eichmann, has no fear that in fact the positions will be thus reversed, so that he will suffer what he is now inflicting on another. The force of the moral argument depends on what they are prepared to allow that it *would* be right to do, even in circumstances which are most improbable. When faced with this argument, they are in a dilemma. If they remain pure nationalists, they are bound to agree that it would not be right for anyone to treat them in the way that they are now treating their victims, if they had the dress, skin and customs of their victims. The pure nationalist's reasons for his actions and recommendations are all, in a sense that I think you will understand, self-centred. The nationalist says: 'It is because a man does not belong to *my* tribe that it is all right to make a victim of him'. The wearing of red or blue beads is quite irrelevant to his real reasons for acting as he does, and the argument we are considering exposes its irrelevance. It is only by ceasing to be a pure nationalist that he can make the wearing of blue beads relevant – by, that is to say, treating the wearing of blue beads as *in itself* of moral relevance, *whoever* is wearing them. To say this is to stop being a nationalist and to become a fanatic about blue beads.

Nationalism as such, therefore, cannot be sustained by trying to treat as morally relevant the differences between nations or tribes. It can only be transmuted into something else, or, as more commonly happens, into a muddled mixture of the two. The something else is what I am calling fanaticism. If you can think of the wearing of blue beads, or a black skin, or a hooked nose, or the having in one's blood a constituent of which these are symptoms, as *in themselves* justifying moral discrimination, even if you were the victim so marked out, then you are immune to the arguments I have so far mentioned.

To illustrate this, let us consider a story (I do not know if it is a true one) which I have heard told about Himmler. It is said that Himmler, after visiting one of the extermination camps which his policy had brought into being, and having seen with his own eyes the terrible things that he had been doing, returned shaken by the experience. But, because he was a fanatic, he got over this feeling of revulsion. In a speech he made afterwards to his subordinates, the story goes, he said that a good Nazi ought not to succumb to these feelings of distaste; there was a duty to be done, and the good Nazi, like any good soldier, ought to be prepared to put up with any experiences, however disagreeable, at the call of duty.[1]

What could lie behind such reasoning? Himmler, we may suppose, like a great many, though not all, Nazis, had an over-riding *ideal* which was stronger than any fellow feeling or humanitarian compunction he might have had about the sufferings he was inflicting on the Jews. To such a person, it would be no use saying 'Suppose it were you that was being treated in that way; would that be right?' He would reply 'Yes it would. The *cause* that I am serving is so important that I am fully prepared that I myself should be sacrificed to further it. There is something about the Jews which is so abominable, so despicable, so harmful to the future of mankind, that it ought to be extirpated from the world at whatever cost to individual men; if I were a Jew, I and all my family and race

[1] I can find no confirmation of this story in *Heinrich Himmler*, by R. Manvell and H. Fraenkel (1965).

ought to be treated in the same way.' There is said to have been a Jew in Austria who actually came to adopt Nazism and to think about his own race as the Nazis did; he ended by committing suicide.

We are dealing now with sentiments which a pure nationalist could never have. For, although nationalism and fanaticism are often combined, and still more often confused, they are quite distinct, and it is most important to understand the difference between them. The nationalist is a person who seeks, to the exclusion of all else, the interests of the group of men to which he belongs. It does not matter to him what qualities the people of this group may or may not possess, or what qualities may or may not be possessed by their enemies. What ties him to the group is simply the fact that he, the individual, belongs to it. If he had been born in Beta instead of in Alpha, the same nationalism would have made him serve devotedly the interests of the Betans, and destroy the Alphans without mercy. The fanatic on the other hand (provided that he is uncontaminated by nationalism) is loyal not to a group of people but to an ideal. He thinks, for example, that some human quality is so desirable that whoever has it, of his own or any other group, ought to be preserved, or so detestable that whoever has it ought to be destroyed; or he thinks that some state of affairs in the world is so superlatively good that it ought to be pursued at whatever cost to anybody, including himself and his nearest and dearest.

Thus we can easily imagine a Chinese at the present time who was moved by pure nationalism; and we can easily imagine one who was moved by pure communist fanaticism. They would be very different. The nationalist would say: 'Let me preserve the interests of China come what may'; the fanatic would say: 'At all costs the revolution must triumph, even if it means the destruction of my country and myself along with it'. When the Chinese government orders the annexation of Tibet or the invasion of India, it is hard to say whether its motives are predominantly nationalistic or predominantly fanatical – for in these cases the same action serves both aims. But the two positions, though often, as I said, combined, are logically quite distinct; they can be combined, as they were by the Nazis, only if it is thought that the members of a particular nation are in fact the embodiment, or the defenders, of the ideal that is being sought. That is why it was so important to the Nazis to make out that the Germans were typical Aryans, and embodied all the Aryan virtues. And that is why it is so important now to the Chinese government to establish that they are the true repository of Marxist orthodoxy.

I said earlier that pure nationalism, in a person who was prepared to think, would be quite easily assailed in argument, but that when combined in this way with fanaticism of some kind it became a much tougher opponent. We can say to a pure nationalist, 'Do you think it would be right for you or for your nation to be treated as you are treating this country?'; and, if he is moved purely by selfish nationalism, he cannot say that it would. But the fanatic can say, 'Yes, if my nation, or I, had the characteristics which make us seek to destroy this other nation, we ought also to be destroyed.' Therefore, while it is admissible to say to the nationalist, 'It can't be right, then, for you to do what you are doing', the fanatic has made this step in the argument impossible.

It may be asked, therefore, whether there are *any* arguments which can compel a fanatic to abandon his fanaticism. My answer to this question is at first sight a pessimistic one: there are no such arguments that can be brought against a real fanatic – a person, that is, who really is prepared to sacrifice everybody's interests, including those of himself and his group, to the pursuit of his ideal. But you will see in a moment that the answer is not so pessimistic as might appear. For the proviso which I have just made – that the person with whom we are arguing should be a *real* fanatic – is satisfied in practice so seldom that we do not need to worry. Real fanatics are so scarce – in spite of appearances to the contrary – that if they were all we had to deal with they would cause us no trouble. Since this may seem a bold assertion to make, in the light of all that has happened in recent years, I will now proceed to defend it.

First, we must be clear, in greater detail, what counts as a real fanatic – that is a man who really is unassailable in argument. By 'unassailable in argument' I mean that he is prepared to argue with us, but that our arguments cannot refute him. There are of course many people who are unassailable in a different sense, in that they just are unable or unwilling to argue; their psychological condition is such, it may be, that our arguments do not reach their minds. No doubt many Nazis were like this, and so are many racialists in other parts of the world today. But since I have no specialist knowledge of psychology, you will not expect me to talk about these people. The fanatic I am concerned with is one who, though prepared to reason, is invincible by reasoning. He, I am maintaining, is a very rare bird indeed.

We must set the stage for such argument by first supposing that all matters of merely factual disagreement have been cleared up. People may be racial fanatics, in a less than strict sense, if they have mistaken ideas about the facts of the racial situation. They may think, for example, that Jews really do carry a factor in their heredity which can be objectively shown to produce results in society of a sort which, if they really were produced, everyone would agree to be harmful. Communist fanatics, in the same loose sense, may be communists because they have certain factual beliefs about, for example, what goes on in free economies. These matters are the province of the geneticist and the economist respectively, and as a philosopher I cannot deal with them. I will suppose, therefore, that in our argument with the fanatic we have reached a stage at which there is a difference of ideals, which has survived agreement about the facts. This is quite possible. A communist and a non-communist may agree that in a free economy a man who has more enterprise, skill and initiative may get a great deal more than an equal share of the goods produced; the non-communist may think this a good thing, the communist an evil thing.

What is it, then, which distinguishes the fanatic, in the strict sense, and makes him immune to our arguments? An ordinary non-fanatical person, if you could prove to him that, say, the collectivisation of agriculture would result in lowered food production *and* lowered living standards for the farmers, would admit that therefore the policy of collectivisation ought to be abandoned. What would a fanatical Stalinist say to this? He might say that the collective way of running farms is inherently better than individual enterprise not because more food is produced or living standards raised (he has admitted that the reverse is true) but because it just is better for farmers to work in co-operation with each other than in competition. He is prepared to push this ideal to the exclusion of other aims, such as the raising of living standards. This means that he puts his ideal of co-operation above the interests of himself and other people.

Let me take a cruder example. Suppose that a South African racialist is convinced that it is an abomination for a black man to mate with a white woman. It is not that he thinks that such alliances result in progeny of lower intelligence, or have other undesirable social consequences. Any beliefs of that sort – factual beliefs – would be open to scientific and factual inquiry; and we have already supposed that such inquiry has been concluded, and that agreement has been reached about the factual consequences of various policies. Our fanatical racialist is not concerned with the consequences of miscegenation; he is concerned with the thing itself, and he thinks it unutterably evil. So evil, that he is prepared to sacrifice the comfort and indeed the lives, not only of the blacks, but of himself and his white friends, in order to prevent miscegenation from taking place. There are such people. He will argue that miscegenation will inevitably occur unless a rigid colour bar is enforced; that its enforcement, given the resentment that this arouses, requires him to give the police arbitrary powers against the blacks and their white sympathisers if order is to be preserved. So he finds himself living in a police state with a gun under his pillow at night and bloody revolution a foreseeable prospect.

Why do I say that such a person is invincible in argument? We have exhausted all factual arguments, and our difference with him remains. Yet the argument which we used against the nationalist, and which was effective against him, will not work with this fanatic. Let us try it on him. We say to him: 'Are you prepared to say that it is right for these measures against miscegenation to be put into force in a state in which you yourself are in the position that the blacks are in now, including being black? If you are not, you cannot say that it is right for you now to adopt these measures; for there cannot be a difference between the rightness of the respective measures unless there is some qualitative difference between the two situations; but this we have supposed there not to be.' The fanatic will, however, reply to this: 'But I am prepared to say that it would be right for this to be done to me if I were in that position; I am prepared to suffer for my ideals; if miscegenation cannot be prevented without people suffering, it must all the same be prevented, even if it is I who suffer.'

Yet another example will show the relevance of all this to the question of peace. Suppose there were a person who thought that Russia was a godless society, in which religion was persecuted; and suppose that he thought that the one overriding duty of the Christian nations of the world was to advance Christianity and make its practice more widespread, for the salvation of as many souls as possible. Such a person might take up an attitude of implacable hostility towards Russia, and, if he were in a position to influence policies in the West, a nuclear war might result. It would be of no use to say to this person: 'If you were a Russian, should the same policies still be pursued towards Russia?' He would say that of course they should; even if he and his whole nation were to be destroyed in a nuclear war – and whatever that nation was, Russia or America or China or Australia – this would be unimportant compared with his objective of making possible the salvation of souls, which can take place as well under a nuclear bombardment as at any other time.

Now, as I said, I have no arguments to offer against people who take up such extreme positions. Why, then, do I say that my conclusion is not pessimistic? Because, when we have seen what it takes to be a fanatic of this extreme sort, we have also seen that such people are likely to be very rare. But now it will be objected that in fact fanatics, of a sort, are not in the least rare; did not the Nazis get enough following to put them in control of almost the whole European continent? How does it come about that extreme racialist policies are successfully pursued in South Africa and in some other places? How did Stalin survive for so long? If there are only a handful of real fanatics, how does it come about that fanatical policies are sometimes adopted by whole nations?

It is easy to answer this question. If all nations were composed of very clear-headed, well-balanced people, in secure circumstances, with full access to the facts through a free and undistorted press, and if, with the aid of philosophers and others, they thought hard and continuously about their nation's policies, and in the end decided on them by majority vote, then there would be no danger at all of fanatical policies getting adopted. In real life it is only too easy. Whole populations can get into a psychological condition in which it is easy for them to be controlled by fanatics. Even if the control is not at first absolute, it can become so through the mastery of the means of propaganda and the suppression of opposition. Nobody needs to be told this. What is not always noticed is that there are also intellectual factors which can help the fanatic to secure the practical and effective support of large numbers of people who are not themselves fanatics. Fanatical policies and the reasons for them are usually presented as an amalgam of many elements. There are all sorts of beliefs about matters of fact – many of them false, but many, it may be, true. There are all sorts of recommendations as to policy, some of which could commend themselves on quite different grounds to a person who was not a fanatic. A reader of *Mein Kampf* might, even if he were himself no Hitler, find in it *some* things of which he could approve – perhaps for purely nationalistic reasons; he might say: 'Whatever you think of Hitler's ideas, he has done wonderfully well for Germany'. It takes more clear-headedness and more application and more disinterestedness than most ordinary men possess to take this amalgam apart. If it were taken apart, then it would be possible to consider the parts separately. And then the false factual beliefs might get shown to be false (for example, it might be clearly demonstrated that the Jews have nothing in their blood which distinguishes them as a race from other men); and others, which were true, might be shown not to have the consequences which the fanatic alleged. And of the policies recommended, it might turn out that some – the ones approved of – could be put into effect without the other fanatical ones; or it might turn out that other policies, when looked at in their nakedness, and deprived of their alleged justification on idealistic grounds, would seem too selfishly nationalistic to be approved.

I cannot conceive of a nuclear war starting now (unless it were by some appalling piece of diplomatic or tactical mismanagement, which is on the whole getting less likely) except through the combination of nationalism and fanaticism in one or more countries. Nationalism by itself would not do to start a major war between world powers, though it still continues to start little wars between smaller powers; for nationalism seeks the interest of a particular country, and no country's interest could today be served by a major war. Fanaticism by itself would not be enough either, because, unless joined with nationalism, it could not get sufficient adherents. War can be prevented, then, if these two attitudes can be disentangled and restrained. How are we to do this? How, that is to say, are we to prevent the spread of fanaticisms which can alone turn nationalism into a serious danger? I said earlier that fanaticism would not get a grip of any country, if the people of that country thought clearly about its policies, had access to the necessary information, and if the will of the majority prevailed. The second and third of these conditions are the ones we hear most about; and they are of course very important. Anything which puts the population of a country either into a condition of ignorance or into one of impotence increases the danger that the rulers of that country will lead it into a war. That is why those old-fashioned freedoms, freedom of the press and freedom to choose the government, must always be defended by those who want peace. But the first condition is important too. It is no use people having information and political power if they are too confused in their thinking to use them right. The intellectual disciplines (philosophy among them) exist to bring about this first condition – clear thinking. That is why freedom to pursue these disciplines – freedom of thought in the widest sense – is the most important freedom of all.

Can anything be said more positively about the attitudes which will prevail in a free and intelligent society among those who are really concerned for the good of the world, and not just their own nation? Is there any middle way between pacifism (the complete renouncement of force of any sort in international affairs) and the war-producing states of mind that I have been discussing? What attitude are we to adopt, in particular, towards the nationalisms and fanaticisms of other countries? If aggressive wars are ruled out, what about defensive ones? And what counts as a defensive war? Perhaps what I have said will clarify these questions a little.

Let us make the assumption, for the sake of simplicity, that in the first instance international action is going to be taken in the main by the existing nation-states. I do not mean to rule out the possibility that in the future there may be truly supranational organs with effective power; but at the moment it looks as if such international organs as we have act only when their members, or a sufficiently powerful group of them, impel them to act. So individual citizens can influence world affairs only through influencing the actions of the state in which they find themselves. The question therefore resolves itself into the question of what kinds of national policies should be advocated and supported by those who are, to a great or small degree, internationally-minded.

The answer becomes clear, in general terms, from what I said earlier. We have first to do all we can to prevent our governments following *nationalistic* policies – by which I mean, really, *selfish* policies. What this means can perhaps now be made clearer. We ought not to support policies of our own government which, if the government of another state were to pursue them in similar circumstances, we are disposed to condemn. It may help if we imagine our own country at the receiving end of such policies. I think that this does give us some sort of guide, when considering such questions as, for example, that of British policy east of Suez. It would lead me to support the actions which our two countries took in relation to the Malaysian-Indonesian confrontation. Equally, it would lead me to condemn the British and French actions during the Suez Canal dispute in 1956. What about Vietnam? I hope that you will not ask me to discuss this question, which depends in part on very difficult factual predictions which I am not qualified to make, and which I have not time to discuss. If the Americans and their allies were seeking purely their own national advantages, I should condemn their actions. If they were pursuing merely some fanatical ideal of anti-communism, I should do likewise. If, on the other hand, they thought that their actions were necessary for the promotion of the good of the people in the region, and were prepared to defend them, even in a case in which their own countries were at the receiving end, I might accept the defence, if the factual predictions on which it was based were correct.

The methodological principle involved in all these decisions is the same; we consider what course of action we can prescribe, taking into account the interests of all the individuals involved, and assigning equal weight to them all. I must emphasise that by 'individuals', I mean 'people', not 'nations'. This principle does not put an absolute bar on a nation trying to conserve its own power, for it may think that there are certain responsibilities which it has in the world, and which it can only fulfil if it is not weakened. If this is so, as it often is, then even an impartial consideration of all the interests involved may lead to the conclusion that this exercise in power politics is justified. For example, I think that Kennedy took the right line during the Cuban missile crisis. On other occasions, as at Suez, it is not justified. Whether it is justified depends partly on whether the end that is aimed at is one that can be commended; but more on whether it is likely to be achieved by that means.

The judgements about the actions of nations to which this sort of reasoning will lead are in the main of the same kind as would be arrived at by utilitarian reasoning. If you like, they are judgements of expediency. I do not believe that there is any conflict between morality and expediency, as so interpreted, though there is often a conflict between the selfish interests of a group and the interests of the whole or of the majority. If it be asked, as it will be, 'What about minorities, and the question of whether it is ever right to override their interests for the sake of the general good?' I should be inclined to give the answer that I would to the same question when it arises in internal politics. This is that in principle it can be right to override the interests of minorities, and that indeed it often is right, and is thought right, and done – as for example when the minority of rich people is subjected to sharply progressive taxation; but that no community will have a healthy and stable existence unless there is a general belief that minorities are going to be, and are, treated justly, according to whatever conception of justice is current in the community – and this may vary. So also in international affairs. The reason why it is not right, even in the general interest, to extinguish a small country against the wishes of its inhabitants, is that in the sort of world in which this is thought of as likely, nobody will feel secure and there will never be stable peace; and that, since peace is overwhelmingly the greatest interest of nearly everyone, such actions cannot possibly be in the general interest. I am of course thinking of cases in which it would be, otherwise, in the general interest to go against the interests of the small nation. When, as in the case of the Nazis and Poland, it is a purely selfish advantage that is being sought, the action is to be condemned on that score alone.

I could say a lot more about this; but I must leave the subject of nationalism and come to fanaticism. My conclusion about nationalism is that, if it is the selfish pursuit of the interests of a group for their own sake, in disregard of the interests of others, it cannot be defended; but that there is still plenty for nations to do which is legitimate and indeed a duty, and which may involve the conservation of their own power. Can we make a similar distinction in relation to fanaticism? To put it crudely, are all crusades ruled out, or only some?

I have time only to state my answer to this question, not to justify it. To do the latter would demand a long excursion into moral philosophy, and indeed into a part of it which is to me still very obscure. Briefly, I would answer that all crusades are ruled out except one – if by 'crusade' we mean the readiness to sacrifice all interests, including our own other interests, to the single-minded pursuit of some cause, however commendable in itself. There can be only one exception to this, and that is when the cause in question is the attempt to do our best for the interests of all, with impartiality, i.e. justice, between persons. To serve *this* cause can never lead us, in the present state of the world, to start aggressive wars, because peace is a major interest of nearly everyone. Any other cause could lead us to start wars; for example, the cause of preventing the spread of communism, or capitalism, or atheism, or any kind of religion, or for that matter the cause of promoting any of these things. For these limited causes, one might start wars, because it is a conceivable policy to sacrifice to these causes the interests (that is to say the other interests) of the greater part of mankind. But to the cause of promoting these interests themselves it is not possible to sacrifice them; this involves a logical contradiction.

My conclusion is, therefore, that the only cause that can engage the wills of clear-thinking people who are trying to do what they ought to do, is the service of mankind as a whole – or, if that be impossible, of the greatest number of them; and that this cause, though it does not commit us to pacifism, rules out the starting of aggressive wars. In nearly all cases this cause has to be furthered through the furtherance of national policies, because nations are at present almost the only source of power. This may not always remain so; but at present all the individual can do is to act through his own country. Therefore, it is of the utmost importance that the policies of states should be arrived at in as rational a way as possible; and an essential condition for this is clear thinking and well-informed public discussion. And it is in promoting these, most of all, that universities like this can contribute to the cause of peace.

8   The Lawful Government[1]

When I was an undergraduate at Balliol before the war, there was another undergraduate there, slightly my senior, who later became a distinguished philosopher; but what was remarkable about him then was that he was a Jacobite. That is to say, he maintained, both in private and on occasion by public demonstration, that the rightful king of England was not George the Sixth (so-called) but a certain Bavarian prince, called, so far as I remember (appropriately) Rupert, and the nearest heir to the Stuart kings.

Shortly after that, when the war began, another acquaintance of mine, a Scottish Nationalist, refused military service on the unusual ground that the Act of Union was not legally binding upon the people of Scotland, since the Scottish Parliament at the time when it was passed was under constraint; and that therefore the present regime had no power to declare war on behalf of Scotland or to require her people to bear arms. He was brought before the courts, whose authority he did not acknowledge, and sent to prison.

These cases are of philosophical interest; for they are only extreme examples of a problem which recurs continually: How does a *de facto* government turn into a *de jure* government? Revolutions are constantly occurring, and the legality of governments is constantly being called in question. Although in this country I have had to go rather far back and give some somewhat bizarre examples, we have only to consider the cases of Iraq, or China, or Russia, or France to see that it is a very

[1] First published in *Philosophy, Politics and Society*, III, ed. Laslett and Runciman (Blackwell, 1967).

This lecture is reprinted in the form in which it was delivered in 1964, and must not be taken as necessarily expressing my present views. In particular, I have not incorporated any discussion of Professor Hart's *The Concept of Law*, which appeared after the lecture was written. I must, however, thank him, and also Professor Alf Ross, for much helpful comment, doubly kind in that they both dissent from many things that I say.

real and practical problem, how the fiats of a group of people who have seized power from the previous government by brute force, contrary to the laws of the previous government, come to be regarded as – even in some sense to *be* – laws binding upon the people of a territory. What decides who *are* the lawful government of the Congo or Vietnam?

I am no lawyer, and shall probably merely succeed in displaying my ignorance of the law in discussing this problem; but nevertheless, since it *is* a philosophical problem and not merely a legal one, I make no apology for attempting a treatment of it, especially since it is a problem which has very close affinities with certain well-known problems in moral philosophy with which I have had a good deal to do.

It is a feature of nearly all attempts to solve this problem that they proceed by looking for a *criterion* of lawfulness in governments. This seems a very natural procedure; for, it might be said, what else could we be after? The problem is that we use this expression 'The lawful government'; it evidently has a meaning; and what else would do as an explanation of its meaning than a statement of the criterion, or the conditions, for calling a government lawful? That this approach to the problem has been thought to be the only one just shows how fatally attractive is the attitude to philosophical analysis which may be called, in the most general sense, *descriptivism*. A descriptivist is a person who thinks that to explain the meaning of any predicate is to give the criteria or conditions which have to be satisfied by a subject before this predicate is correctly predicated of it. I need not now rehearse the many mistakes that have been caused in other branches of philosophy (especially moral philosophy) by this assumption; we shall see that in the philosophy of law it has been just as damaging. If you want an example to show that descriptivism won't do, I will give perhaps the most hackneyed one: in order to understand the meaning of 'I promise' it is not sufficient or necessary to know what criteria or conditions have to be fulfilled by me before I can properly say 'I promise'.

Let us then, bearing this general point in mind, consider some of the stock solutions to the problem of the meaning of the expression 'lawful government'. First and most obvious we have what may be called the 'Might is Right' solution. This name is a bit unfair, as we shall see; but it will do. According to this view, the criterion of lawfulness is this: if a group of people (called the government) is able to enforce its will upon the people of a territory, then it is the lawful government of that territory, and its enactments are binding laws. Anybody who breaks these laws is then a criminal (or tortfeasor, etc.). And that is all there is to be said. This solution solves the problem by denying that there is any real difference between *de facto* and *de jure* governments. It is by far the simplest solution.

The phrase 'Might is Right' is, however, as I said, unfair. For 'Right' is naturally taken to mean 'morally right'; and this introduces a red herring, which puts this view at an unfair disadvantage. Of course it is most implausible (to put it no stronger) to suggest that whatever a government *can* do, it is morally right for it to do. So a proponent of this view might justly protest that we ought to leave morals out of it; he is not talking about morals, but about laws. Whatever may be the moral issues involved, and whether the laws made by the government are morally good or bad, the question whether they are *legally* binding is simply the question whether the government has the power to secure general obedience to them. On this view (which is very plausible) we say that Mr Kosygin's regime, and not the descendants of the Tsar (if any), is the lawful government of Russia simply because its writ runs in Russia and theirs does not.

But there are well-known objections to this view. If a group of brigands seizes power in, say, Panama, and makes a lot of regulations for the conduct of the people of Panama, does it by that fact alone become the lawful government of Panama? If this were so, then a number of questions which manifestly do trouble us would not do so. The citizens of Panama, and foreign governments, ask themselves questions like 'Is this the lawful government of Panama?' and hesitate about the answer. But if the writ of the brigands runs, then what further question can there be of this nature, according to the theory which we are considering? Suppose that I am a Panamanian supporter of the previous regime; is it logically absurd for me to say 'Yes, I know that these brigands have the power to put in prison or to shoot anybody who breaks their regulations; but nevertheless the whole procedure is quite unlawful'? Suppose that people who think like this band together, and perhaps enlist the assistance of a foreign power, and overthrow the brigands. They will then no doubt declare that the acts of the brigands were illegal. But, on the 'Might is Right' theory, this would be a manifest falsehood; for, during the five years, say, that the brigands enjoyed power, their writ *did* run in Panama; and therefore, on the theory, their enactments *were* binding laws. The theory, by denying a distinction which we require to make, that between power and legal authority, makes nonsense of the whole conception 'legally binding'. It may of course be that the conception *is* nonsense – or at any rate is nonsense when applied in unsettled circumstances like those we have been describing. But it would be hasty to draw this pessimistic conclusion before we have examined some other solutions. If we say that it is altogether nonsense, we shall be up against the objection that people seem to use it quite satisfactorily and to make themselves understood; but if we say that it is nonsense under unsettled conditions, but sense under normal conditions, we shall have on our hands a very difficult demarcation problem – not perhaps an insoluble one, but one which, in view of the examples with which I started, one does not want to have to face if one hasn't got to.

We might try to modify the 'Might is Right' theory in order to get over these objections. An attractive modification is to say that it isn't enough for a group of people to have the power to enforce their will; there must be something which is recognisable as a *legal system*. So if we find a brigand leader shooting people who don't do what he says, that isn't enough to make his commands laws; there have to be enactments couched in a universal form, with recognisable and consistent procedures for making and enforcing them, including a legislature, courts of law with judges, etc. Where there is such a system, we say that those enactments are legally binding which are used in making decisions, giving verdicts, etc., by the courts. But this is still a recognisable version of the 'Might is Right' theory, because all these conditions are not sufficient, even on the revised version of the theory, unless the system does command the power to enforce its enactments. One could have all the rest of the conditions (some people making enactments and others condemning and sentencing people they called criminals, and so on); but if the 'criminals' always went scot free, because the courts had no power to enforce their sentences, then, on this theory, there would not be a legal system, and the so-called 'laws' would not be binding.

Now here we must carefully distinguish between two questions: the question 'Is there a legal system in such and such a territory?' and the question 'Are the enactments of the system legally binding on the inhabitants of the territory?' I think that most people would be prepared to agree that, if all the conditions which I have just listed are fulfilled in a territory, there is a legal system in that territory. But the cases of the Jacobite and the Scottish Nationalist with which I started ought to make us see that it is possible, without contradiction, to admit that there is a legal system in this sense, but to deny that its enactments are legally binding. The Scottish Nationalist was put in prison; but was his contention that the court did not have authority over him empirically refuted by pointing to all these judges sitting up in big chairs wearing wigs, and all the policemen and warders and hangmen doing what the judges say? He would surely reply 'Yes, I agree that a very exact travesty of the form of law is being put on; but that doesn't make the procedures any more lawful; for all these judges, etc., are appointed by a government which owes its power to an act of unlawful force perpetrated upon the lawful Scottish parliament in 1707'. Whether or not we agree about the historical facts upon which he is relying, we surely cannot deny that a similar argument brought forward by a French Royalist or a Russian Tsarist would have considerable weight against the theory which we are discussing. The mere existence of a legal system, as described, does not constitute its legality, in the sense of 'lawfulness'.

I conclude that even this modification of the 'Might is Right' theory will not save it. Force does not become law by disguising itself in the trappings of law. But since I am more interested in the general defect of all descriptivist theories of law, I will now go on to mention other examples of such theories. We may consider next the theory often known as 'popular sovereignty'. According to this, a government is lawful if it enjoys the support of the people of a territory. If there is a revolution in a territory, then the revolutionary group becomes the lawful government if and when, and only if and when, the people of the territory acknowledge it as the government – which acknowledgement they give, either in words, or more commonly by acquiescing in or more positively supporting the acts of the group.

It is not all that easy to distinguish this theory from the modified form of the 'Might is Right' theory which I have just been discussing. There is nevertheless a crucial difference; for it is not an analytic truth, but a contingent fact, that it is impossible for a government to survive for long without popular support. An up-to-date tyrant, equipped with the latest military and psychological machinery, might continue indefinitely to *impose his will* on the inhabitants, in the sense that they obeyed his regulations; yet such a person would not be said to enjoy their support. He would, indeed, have to lead the operators of the machinery 'like men by their opinion' (as Hume put it[1]); but that does not affect my point. So, in such a situation, the modified 'Might is Right' theory would call the tyrant the lawful government, but the 'Popular Sovereignty' theory would not. And this difference is very important.

Next we must consider two descriptivist theories which, though like the two we have just considered in that they too seek to explain the meaning of 'lawful government' by giving a criterion for its application, differ from them in that the criterion offered is of a more elusive character. I will call these the 'Hereditary' theory and the 'Natural Law' theory. The hereditary theory is now old-fashioned, but was once almost universally accepted. According to it, a lawful government is one consisting of a legitimate ruler (or, in exceptional cases, rulers). A ruler is legitimate if he is the rightful heir of a legitimate ruler. Now there are certain well-known difficulties in this theory – theoretical difficulties which give rise to very real practical ones, and are in fact the main reason why this theory has lost its appeal. I mean difficulties about how we determine what are the rules of rightful succession, and – more serious – about how the *first* legitimate ruler became legitimate.

These indeterminacies in the theory are symptomatic of a deeper defect, as we shall see. They have often led to the hereditary theory being backed up by an appeal to the natural law theory, which we must now consider. It might be suggested that questions of who is the legitimate ruler, and what are the laws of rightful succession, since they cannot without circularity be determined by the ordinary laws of the territory, might be

[1] *Essay IV.*

determined by appeal to a natural law above all actual human laws. And such appeals were often made (e.g. by Sir Robert Filmer to whom Locke replied).

Without entering into the details of this question, I should like to point out the main distinctions between what may be called 'empirical' descriptivist theories of law (like the first two we considered) and what may be called 'non-empirical' descriptivist theories (like the last two). Empirical theories give a tolerably determinate criterion of lawfulness in governments; we can at any rate make a decent show of determining whether the criterion is satisfied by a given government. The cost of this determinacy is that the theories are easily shown to be absurd; it is obvious that we use the expression 'lawful government' in a different way from that which these theories claim. This can be shown by pointing out that it is not self-contradictory to say that a certain government has the power to impose its will, but deny that it is the lawful government; and that it is not self-contradictory to say that a government has the support of the people but is not the lawful government. Such theories are *obviously* absurd, once one has had this pointed out, because the phrases to which they make the expression 'lawful government' equivalent have a more or less determinate meaning, and this is clearly not the same as that of the *definiendum*.

Non-empirical descriptivist theories, in a conscious or unconscious attempt to evade this kind of refutation, introduce into their *definientia* expressions whose meaning is sufficiently indeterminate for us not to be able to say with certainty whether or not they are equivalent to a given expression. This makes theories of this kind sufficiently slippery to elude the kind of refutation made popular by Moore of which we have just given examples. But it lays these theories open to another charge, that of saying nothing definite at all. They claim to give a criterion of lawfulness, but leave it entirely unclear what falls under this criterion and what does not. Thus, suppose that, for example, there is a dispute about whether a certain kingdom can pass in the female line. Now there might, of course, be already in 'existence' a law of succession which determined this question. It would not determine it finally, for the reason (circularity) already alluded to, which will become even plainer as we proceed. But for the moment let us suppose that there is no such law. We may then find the two parties both appealing to the natural law. One of them, fingering the pages of Aristotle's *Politics*, may claim that woman is naturally unfitted to rule a kingdom, and that therefore the kingdom cannot be inherited in the female line; the other party may claim that woman is naturally the equal of man. How could such a dispute possibly be settled? Here, as to wider issues, we may apply the remark of the distinguished Danish jurist Alf Ross that 'like a harlot, natural law is at the disposal of everyone. The ideology does not exist that cannot be defended by an appeal to the law of nature' (*On Law and Justice*, p. 261).

I will now turn to an attempt to give a more satisfactory account than those which I have so far discussed. And in order to do so I shall import from moral philosophy a device which has proved of some assistance there. This is the distinction between so-called 'first-order' moral judgements and so-called 'inverted-commas' moral judgements. It would be out of place here to try to explain what is meant by a first-order moral judgement; this class includes most of the typical moral judgements that we make. I am concerned only with the relation between these and the 'inverted-commas' moral judgements. An inverted-commas moral judgement is true if and only if some first-order moral judgement is actually made by some determinate or at least roughly determinable set of people. For example, there is a use of the sentence 'We ought to call on the Joneses' such that it does not express a first-order moral judgement of our own, but only the judgement that our calling on the Joneses is required in order to conform to the moral judgements made by a certain set of people, viz. those known as 'polite society'.

This distinction is even more applicable to the field of law than it is to the field of morals – and has indeed been frequently made use of in other terms. There is a school of jurists who, in seeking to define 'lawful' by giving a *criterion* of lawfulness (the programme of all those theories which I am criticising), think that they can achieve this object by treating all legal statements as if they were inverted-commas legal statements. This is the origin of the well-known theory that 'the law is what the courts will decide'. Now this theory might seem at first sight an adequate account of legal statements made by certain classes of people: for example, law dons instructing their pupils, solicitors advising their clients, and counsel giving counsel's opinion. It is, however, as has been pointed out in a justly famous article by Professor Hart,[1] an inadequate account of declarations of what is or is not the law made by judges giving their judgements in court. For the judges are then not *predicting* what the courts *will* or *would* decide; they are themselves deciding. It may be all right to interpret a solicitor's advice in an inverted-commas way as a statement which is true if and only if the courts would make a certain first-order judgement if the case were put to them; but the inverted-commas judgement cannot be fully explained unless an explanation is forthcoming of the first-order judgement. Any attempt to explain *this* as an inverted-commas judgement lands us in circularity or in regress. I am ignoring, for the sake of simplicity, the complications introduced by the existence of higher and lower courts.

Professor Hart, in the article to which I have referred, called the judgements of courts 'ascriptive', to distinguish them from ordinary descriptive judgements such as the statements of solicitors may be. It may be all right to say that if a solicitor says that a certain piece of land is my property, he is (in a wide philosophical sense) describing it; for he is stating that that land possesses a certain relational characteristic, namely that if I claim in court to be protected in certain ways in the enjoyment of it, the protection will be forthcoming. But the court, in giving me this protection, is not *describing* the land in any sense; rather, it is *instructing* the police and all whom it may concern to preserve my enjoyment of the land.

Hart does not in this article (which is concerned chiefly with the notion of responsibility) pursue the question of how these ideas are to be applied to problem-situations such as are created by revolutions, *coups d'état* and the like. It seems to me, however, that we cannot stop just where Hart leaves the matter. He considers only what is the case where we have a settled regime, and where it is clear to all (*given*, we might almost say) what persons sitting in what places are properly referred to as 'the courts'. But in revolutions this ceases to be the case. And it seems to me that the fact that it ceases to be the case in revolutions reveals a gap in our account of what

[1] 'The Ascription of Responsibility and Rights', in *Logic and Language, First Series*, ed. A. G. N. Flew.

happens even in settled times. For, as the examples with which I started show, it is possible even in settled times for somebody without self-contradiction to challenge the lawfulness – or the authority or competence – of the 'courts' which (he admits) are generally *accepted* as lawful, or of the regime of which they are a part. And we have to think what we could say to such a person.

If a solicitor says that a certain piece of land is my property, it may be that he means that if I went before a lawfully constituted court, I should be protected in the enjoyment of this land. And the same will apply, *mutatis mutandis*, if a Scottish Nationalist goes to *his* solicitor and asks him whether Her Majesty's 'government' have lawful authority to require him to bear arms. But what happens if the Scottish Nationalist asks his solicitor what is the lawfully constituted court of supreme jurisdiction for Scotland? The solicitor will no doubt say that the House of Lords is; but what does he mean by this? Perhaps we can interpret it, as before, to mean that if the question is put, in due form, to the lawfully constituted court of supreme jurisdiction, it will say, 'The House of Lords is the lawfully constituted court of supreme jurisdiction'. For short, 'The lawful supreme court will say "The House of Lords is the lawful supreme court"'. But this will obviously not satisfy the Scottish Nationalist. For if he does not acknowledge that the House of Lords is the lawful supreme court, it is no use telling him that the *House of Lords* will say 'The House of Lords is the lawful supreme court'. This would not be, in his eyes, the judgement of a lawful court at all (in a case concerning Scotland), let alone that of the lawful supreme court. He would only acknowledge as the lawful supreme court for Scotland some Scottish court, which perhaps does not at the present time exist. So anything that his solicitor could say to him is quite irrelevant to his question. The solicitor can only report or predict what other people have said or would say; he cannot make a first-order legal judgement. And of all the people who *can* make first-order legal judgements, we can ask '*Quo jure?*' – a question which cannot be answered, without circularity, by appealing to the same courts for a pronouncement upon their own competence or authority.

So, then, we are left in an apparently inescapable *impasse*. If we say that all legal statements are inverted-commas statements, we make their meaning altogether inexplicable, since inverted-commas statements of any kind cannot be interpreted unless we know the meaning of the corresponding first-order statements. But if we admit any first-order legal statements, the question arises, How do we know who is competent to pronounce them? And since the statement that somebody is competent is itself a legal statement, this question seems unanswerable without circularity.

The way out of this impasse, as it seems to me, is to recognise that *there is no reason to confine the notion of ascription to what is said by courts*. There are, that is to say, some uses of words like 'lawful', even by ordinary people and not judges, which have to be called 'ascriptive'. These ascriptive uses by ordinary people are in settled times not common; but their existence or at least possibility has to be acknowledged if we are to understand other uses of the terms which are parasitic upon them. In unsettled times they become quite common.

Let me first give examples of such uses in unsettled times. Let us suppose that there is a revolution in progress (for example, a republican revolution against a monarchy), and that it is as yet uncertain which side will win. We may then find one side saying things like 'The King's government is the lawful government of this country', and the other side saying 'The King is a tyrant; the lawful government is one resting upon the will of the people'. Now it is most important to notice that, odd as it may at first sight seem, these two sets of people may *mean the same* by the word 'lawful'; indeed, they must mean the same, if these two utterances are to express a disagreement between them. The monarchists emphatically do not *mean* by 'lawful', 'set up by the rightful heir of a legitimate monarch'; and the republicans do not mean 'supported by the people'. Otherwise their utterances would be reduced to something near triviality. They are judgements of substance, and in substantial disagreement with each other. And they are not inverted-commas judgements; the parties are not saying that somebody else would or will judge in a certain way; they are themselves doing some judging. In fact, in a revolutionary situation like this, since any judge is, as it were, tainted by adherence to one side or the other, and since, therefore, legality cannot be established by appeal to judges, every man has to be his own judge, and ascribe to one government or the other the right to be called the lawful government. We may call this kind of ascriptive performance an *act of allegiance*. That is what, in a revolutionary situation, the declaration that a certain government is lawful amounts to. The revolution may be said to be over (*de facto*) when the bulk of the population (or of that part of it which is capable of influencing affairs) has come over to one side by implicitly or explicitly declaring its allegiance.

There is another kind of judgement of legality which we must notice which takes place at times of revolution – that made by foreign governments. They have in the end to recognise one side or the other as the lawful government of the territory. When they do this they are not describing the government – they are not saying that it possesses a certain feature named lawfulness. They are doing what they are said to be doing – performing an act of recognition, which is one kind of ascription. It would be inappropriate to say, 'No, your statement that it is the lawful government is false; the government does not have the feature called lawfulness'.

Notice that it is not, at any rate normally, any Tom, Dick or Harry in the United States that has to decide whether Mao's government is the lawful government of China. The United States has a government acknowledged by its citizens as lawful; and its citizens cannot at one and the same time acknowledge it as lawful, and make for themselves independent judgements about what is the lawful government of China. For part of what they are doing in acknowledging as the lawful government of the U.S. the government of Johnson is to depute to Johnson and his government the task of recognising or refusing to recognise foreign governments as lawful. So, as we should expect, the status of the citizens of the U.S. is different in this respect from the status of the citizens of China whose government is the object of the act of recognition. The citizens of China recognise (or, better, give their allegiance to) their government directly, having nobody else to depute the act to; the citizens of the U.S. recognise it, if they do, only indirectly, by acknowledging the U.S. government as the proper body to do it (or refuse to do it) on their behalf.

At this point I must warn you against a common misinterpretation. If I do not warn you, somebody may attribute to me the view that the following statement is analytic: 'Whatever government is given allegiance by the bulk of the people of a

country is the lawful government'. At least, this commonly
happens in the corresponding controversy in moral philosophy.
This is not what I mean; indeed this view is a descriptivist view
of just the sort I have been attacking, very similar to the one I
called the popular sovereignty theory. It is an attempt to give
an inverted-commas account of a first-order legal judgement,
and, like all such attempts, is destined to prove abortive. Only
in an inverted-commas sense could 'the lawful government' be
the equivalent of 'the government to whom the bulk of the
people gives allegiance'; for the latter expression means much
the same as 'the government *called* "the lawful government"
by the bulk of the people'. If this were what it meant, we should
have an infinite regress on our hands, in that the *definiendum*
recurs in the *definiens*, and thus the *definiens* can be infinitely
expanded (without illuminating us in the least) by substituting
the *definiens* for the occurrence of the *definiendum* inside itself.
This absurdity is not what I am suggesting. What I am saying
is that some statements of the form 'So and so is the lawful
government' are themselves acts of allegiance, not that they are
equivalent to statements that somebody has performed or
would perform acts of allegiance.

Nevertheless, though my own theory is to be emphatically
distinguished from the popular sovereignty theory, I may
perhaps claim that it does restate correctly the truth which
was incorrectly stated by that theory. In moral philosophy,
similarly, my own view is often confused with the view called
'subjectivism'; I would claim, however, that my own view
does state correctly a truth which subjectivism tries to state
but lands in falsehood. But I won't digress into moral philosophy.

I must also utter another warning, because there is another
objection that is sure to be made. It will be said that I have
given a purely 'emotive' account of legal judgements, reducing
them to mere shouts like '*Vive la république!*' This is not my
intention. I hope it is not now generally thought, as it used to
be, that if an utterance is not descriptive, it must be a mere
expression of feeling.

There is, however, a legitimate objection which might be
made to what I have said so far – in fact several. The first is
this: You have maintained, it might be said, that, in certain
contexts (especially revolutionary ones), the expression 'The

lawful government' is to be understood as the key phrase in an act of recognition or of allegiance; but this explains nothing until you tell us what these things called allegiance and recognition are that are being expressed. The second objection is that I have not said whether there are (as there are generally thought to be) any *reasons* which entitle us to give or withhold recognition or allegiance; surely, it may be said, if they are just acts that we can perform or not perform, why shouldn't we, on your theory, just toss a coin. Surely, though, argument is in place here: whether to give allegiance or recognition is a difficult question; you make it sound too easy. And of course somebody will go on from there to suggest that I have put the cart before the horse – the only sufficient and necessary reason for giving allegiance or recognition to a government is that it is the lawful government; first we have to establish the *fact* that it is the lawful government, and then, when we have established that, we can recognise it. The third objection is the following: It may be allowed that I have made out my case with regard to revolutionary situations; but it may be maintained that in settled conditions there is nothing to correspond to all this.

Let us consider these objections in turn. The first is: What is recognition or allegiance? I will answer simply, but in the knowledge that a lawyer would add a good deal of complications and refinements. First, recognition. A foreign power, in recognising a government, is according to that government certain rights, especially rights over the citizens of the recognising power; these rights then become enforceable through the courts of the recognising power. Thus an act of recognition may be interpreted as an instruction, rather like an ordinary piece of legislation, to the courts of the recognising power to treat the recognised power and its citizens in certain determined ways. The recognising power also, in the act of recognition, declares its readiness to enter into diplomatic relations of the normal sort. There are no doubt other elements in recognition which an international lawyer would list. Allegiance is something different. In giving my allegiance to a certain government, I am committing myself to treat its regulations as laws binding upon myself; that is to say, I am submitting or subjecting myself to it. After I have made such an act of allegiance, or acknowledged it to be the lawful government, I can no longer complain if the government, in pursuance of its laws, puts me into prison (or rather, though I can complain, as any citizen can complain if he considers the laws unjust, I cannot make a certain kind of complaint, namely the kind of complaint that I might make if brigands kidnapped me and kept me confined against my will). I do not think that I can at the moment give any clearer explanation than that.

The second objection is about what are the reasons for giving or withholding allegiance or recognition. The answer is that there are plenty of reasons, only they are not *legal* reasons. The position is a little similar (though there are important differences) to that in which a body of people form a club. There may be many reasons for forming a club – the desire to play cricket, or to undertake concerted action against one's employers, or many other reasons. To form a club is to incur certain obligations; but one does not form the club *because* one has the obligations. Similarly, to give one's allegiance to a government is to lay upon oneself certain obligations; but one does not, in asking whether one shall give one's allegiance, ask first whether one has the obligations, and, if one has, give the allegiance. The reasons for giving one's allegiance to a government are of many kinds. It may be the desire to have protection; or the desire to promote a state of society of which one approves; or the desire to have a government which supports a religion to which one adheres. Some of these reasons are moral ones, some prudential, some political, and some perhaps of other kinds. None of them is a legal reason.

The case with recognition is similar. There are many reasons for recognising or refusing to recognise a foreign government, but none of them is a legal reason. It may be that recognition is refused because, since it does not control the territory, recognition would be pointless (it has not the power to discharge those obligations which are normally demanded in return for recognition). Or perhaps it is considered politically or even morally objectionable. Or perhaps it is merely that withholding recognition is thought to be a good move in power politics. But there is never, strictly speaking, a legal reason. For there to be a legal reason, the recognising power would have to be able to say 'This government is the lawful government of the territory; therefore we hereby recognise it as the lawful government'. But this would be like saying 'You are my deputy, therefore I appoint you my deputy'; or 'This ship is called the *Queen Mary*, therefore I name her the *Queen Mary*'.

Put thus baldly, however, my thesis makes declarations of recognition and allegiance a bit too like legislation, and not like enough to judgements of the courts. It would be true to say that there cannot be legal reasons for enacting pieces of legislation (i.e. one cannot say, 'This is the law, therefore I make it the law' – though natural-law jurists talk as if this were what one ought to do). So we require to qualify the doctrine. It is a matter of dispute among jurists to what extent judges *find in* an already existing law what they declare to be the law in difficult cases, and to what extent they actually *make* the law. It seems to me that the latter is at least sometimes the case. But it would be obviously wrong to maintain that it is always the case. Now acts of recognition in particular are or ought to be guided by principle and precedent in the same sort of way as judgements of the courts are in difficult cases. So it might be said that, although no specific legal reasons can be given for recognition, there is a body of legal precedent and principle which tells us when we ought to recognise a new government in a country which has had a revolution. In the case of allegiance, I do not think that there is any such body of legal precedent or principle – though there are obvious political and prudential and moral principles which might guide us. I do not think that these qualifications to my thesis make it altogether nebulous.

This second objection has been put to me in an even stronger form (privately) by Professor Hart. He says that 'it is the function of international law to provide legal reasons [for recognising or not recognising governments as lawful]: a government with general support and ordered control, after extinction of hopes of restoration of the displaced *de jure* government, may have a right to recognition'. This form of the objection raises the general question of the status of international law, into which I shall not have time to go. Briefly, the fundamental question seems to me to be, What makes international law the law? Not, certainly, the opinions of international lawyers; they cannot, any more than solicitors, determine what international law is to be; they can only try to say what it is. International law, it seems to me, has at any rate no stronger a position than the English common law, which depends on the accumulation of precedents. And the precedents in this case are past recognitions, etc., by sovereign states. So the situation remains as I described it.

The third objection is the most difficult to meet. This admits, for the sake of argument, that what I say about revolutionary situations is correct, but challenges me to produce anything going on in ordinary settled situations which could possibly be called 'acts of allegiance'. When faced with this objection, I am bound to admit that I do not know of any occasion in settled regimes in which anybody uses expressions like 'So-and-so is the lawful government of this country' as a declaration of allegiance. I can very well imagine, however, that such a form of words might be used if it were desired to have a test of allegiance or loyalty for candidates for office or army officers; and indeed there are forms of words in attestations, etc., which are reminiscent of this. It does not, however, particularly matter what people say; what we want to get at is something that they must all *think*, if they are loyal citizens. To be loyal to a certain regime is to acknowledge it as the source of binding laws, whether the acknowledgement is done verbally or not. If anybody does not acknowledge the government of his country as the source of laws binding upon himself, then he is, at least at heart, a rebel. And this, indeed, is all that can be said to the Scottish Nationalist and the Jacobite.

The view which I wish to contest may be caricatured as follows. If I am brought before the magistrates to be charged with a parking offence a friend may say to me, 'Do you acknowledge the lawful authority of the court to try you?' According to the view which I am contesting, if I reply, 'Yes', all I am doing is to make a statement of fact to the effect that this court is set up in accordance with laws which higher courts in fact use in making their judgements; that its judgements, if they do not contain what the higher courts judge to be legal errors, will not be reversed by those higher courts simply because of the constitution of the magistrate's court. In short, I am saying that this court is acknowledged as having lawful authority by the courts of this country. But on my view I should be meaning more than this. *I* should be acknowledging the authority of the court over me. I should be doing something that a Scottish Nationalist, for example, might not do (though he might do all that, on the view of my opponents, I am doing). The Scottish Nationalist may readily make inverted-commas acknowledgements of lawfulness; but it may be that he will not, as I will, make first-order ones.

Of course I might only be using the expression in an inverted-commas way. Compare the following situation: I say to somebody in a letter that so-and-so is my agent; this may be a mere statement of fact to the effect that I have appointed so-and-so as my agent; but it is much more likely to be taken as an act *committing* me to be bound by whatever so-and-so does in my name.

The non-descriptive, first-order character of such utterances comes out much more strongly when they are negated. If the Scottish Nationalist said, 'I do not acknowledge the authority of this court to try me' or 'This court is not a lawfully-constituted court', he would clearly not be making a factual statement to the effect that the authority of this court would not be upheld by higher courts. He would be refusing to submit to the authority of the court.

The ordinary citizen, in settled times, does not need to go about performing acts of allegiance or acknowledgement of the lawful authority of courts or governments. It is taken for granted that as a loyal citizen he acknowledges their authority. And since he does this, it is left to them, acting as the special organs for declaring what the law is or what it is to be, to make laws (in the case of governments) and interpret and enforce them (in the case of the courts).

I have been speaking hitherto in a very loose way in characterising *what* it is which is recognised, or to which allegiance is given, or which is acknowledged to be lawful. I have used expressions like 'the government' and 'the regime', and have treated the courts as if they were a part of these. I do not now wish to go into the complications of constitutional theory, and should only reveal my ignorance if I did. Nor do I wish to discuss at length the so-called problem of sovereignty. It is obvious that many difficult problems remain to be dealt with, with which I am not competent to deal. But may I end by restating my position in the barest possible outline? To acknowledge a government or regime as lawful is not, when this is a first-order judgement, to state any *facts* about it; in particular, it is not to state the fact that there are courts and that these *call* the government lawful, and use the laws made by it in their judgements. For we could acknowledge all this, and still call the monarch (supposing that he was a monarch) who made these laws a *pretender*; and

> Who pretender is, and who is king,
> God bless us all, that's *quite another thing*.

9 Community and Communication

What are cities and what are they for?

If we ask, in Socratic fashion, 'What is a city?', it is tempting to answer, in the fashion of Le Corbusier, 'A city is a machine for *communicating* in'. But 'machine' would be wrong. A city is not a machine. It is not normally designed; it grows. Often you cannot stop it growing. When things go wrong with cities, they are less like the breakdowns which affect machines than like the diseases which afflict animals and plants. The town planner is not like an engineer (he cannot *repair* a city like a motor-car); he is like a doctor looking after a living organism, which he keeps healthy if he can, or, if he cannot, tries to restore it to health – by surgery if he must. But even surgery is not like repairing a car; the organism has to grow well again after you have interfered with it. The car comes back from the garage as good as it was before the trouble started; when the man comes back from hospital it may be months before he is really well again.

Or we might say that town planning is like gardening. Even in the literal sense gardening is an important part of it – such as the landscape gardening of genius which has redeemed the mostly second-rate architecture of Canberra, and made it a fine city in spite of itself. But even when he is planting not trees but people, the town planner has, like the gardener, to plant and pray. How the thing that he has planted thrives, he can to some extent influence by the care he gives it; but it is largely out of his control. For all that, there are good and bad gardeners. The planner's contribution is important. He cannot leave everything to nature. As the old gardener said to his pious

Written as an introductory essay for the conference 'People and Cities' at Coventry in 1968, and first published in *People and Cities*, ed. S. Verney (Fontana Books, 1969).

master, 'You ought to see what the garden gets like after God has had it to himself for a bit'. And there is an important difference between cities and gardens: plants, if badly looked after, just die; human beings protest and rebel. So you had better respect their feelings, if you want their co-operation.

Let us say, then, that a city is, not a machine, but an *organism for communication*. Why 'for communication'? Let us imagine a country whose inhabitants do not live in cities, or even in villages (which are a kind of small cities), but spread out in their houses at equal intervals all over the countryside. Of what would they be deprived? They can grow food and eat it, they can grow cotton and wool and clothe themselves, and they can build houses. They can also exploit such mineral resources as do not require the co-operation of large numbers of people to mine them. What will they *not* be able to do because they do not have cities or villages? The answer is that, generally speaking, they cannot communicate. There may be a postal service (but where did they learn to write?), or even a telephone service (but the telephone was invented and perfected in cities), or radio and television (whose stations, however, are nearly always centred on cities). But they cannot go and shop (shopping is one form of communication; its essence is an agreement to exchange money for goods, and to reach an agreement, we have to communicate). They cannot have a government (all forms of government, however tyrannical, are forms of communication; laws, for example, are pieces of language telling people what they have to do; and language is communication). That is why it is difficult to conceive of government without a seat of government – that is, a capital city. To govern, it is necessary for people to *come together* and talk to each other.

The reason why it is almost impossible to have either commerce or government without cities is that both are forms of communication, and communication of nearly all kinds involves people coming together, which they cannot do unless they have somewhere to come to. The same is true of the arts. The people in my imaginary country without cities would be extremely unlikely to develop any arts worth mentioning; nearly all arts depend on either a market or an audience, and you cannot have either of these things unless people come to-gether. Art is a form of communication; it depends on their being people to communicate with. This applies especially to architecture. You are unlikely to get fine buildings put up in a city in which communications have broken down.

Commerce; government; art: all these kinds of communication largely depend on the existence of cities. But we need now to ask more precisely what we mean by 'communication'. It will at once become evident that we mean more than one thing. First of all there is communication in the crudest physical sense: the sense in which 'Communications' appears as one of the chapter headings in almost any city planner's report. The chapter is usually the one which excites the most controversy, and on it, usually, everything else in the plan depends. Physical communications are, indeed, a means, not an end; but they are an essential means if the city is to function. If shoppers find it too inconvenient to get to the shops, or if the shopkeepers find it too expensive to get their goods from the wholesaler or factory, the shopping centre declines. If members of parliament miss important votes because they are held up in traffic blocks, or if civil servants are late for committees of which they are essential members – or if, as in New Delhi, the clerks in the offices have to exhaust themselves every morning and evening bicycling for miles and miles up Lutyens' magnificent vistas, or, as in London, cram themselves into trains which cannot be relied on – government and commerce cannot function well. Nor can the arts, if you cannot be sure of arriving on time for a concert or a play.

This is not an argument for or against any particular mode of transport. There are many modes; but whatever modes are adopted, they must enable people to come into and travel within a city with reasonable convenience in order to communicate with one another – for that is what the city is for. And in so doing, they must not make it impossible for other people to do *their* communicating. These other people, too, live in communities, which must not be divided by streams of traffic; if they are, communication between one side of the street and the other will become dangerous, and there will be so much noise that verbal communication is difficult anywhere near the street.

But physical communication, or transport, is not an end in itself. When I am sitting by myself in my car, I am not communicating, but only trying to get somewhere in order to communicate with somebody. One of the chief difficulties

facing those who govern cities is to decide the relative importance of the communication that different people are trying to
achieve by coming into cities. Professor Buchanan has stressed
that, if we want a reasonable standard of environment in our
cities (which means, at least, an environment which makes
human communication easy), the amount of transport we can
have coming in to and going out of them (the accessibility, as
he calls it) will depend on what we can afford to spend, and in
many cases will be limited even then. So we have to distinguish
between essential and inessential traffic. And this means
distinguishing between those whose journeys are really necessary and those whose journeys are not. But how can we do this
without an assessment of the importance of the communication
which is the object of the journey? Who is to make this value
judgement? Here are two people stuck in two different traffic
jams going into the same city centre to meet one another: how
important is it that they should succeed?

The bigger a city is, the more intractable these problems
become, as has been shown mathematically by the work of
Professor Smeed and others. This has led to the demand that
we should limit the size of cities – if only we could! Probably
the most helpful approach is to ask what forms of communication are essential to the life of a particular city as an organism
for communication, and to offer the other forms incentives to
transfer elsewhere. For example, in London and other big cities
many firms have moved their main offices to the suburbs; and
the same thing has happened to shopping centres in many
places. The proposal has even been made to move the seat of
government of this country to Yorkshire. It is obvious that if
the federal capital of the United States had been in New York,
the problems of that city would have been even more difficult
than they are. To move a seat of government may be intended
not merely to ease the traffic problems in the city it leaves, but
to improve communications with the region it goes to, as in
the case of Brasilia. To some extent, cities can specialise with
respect to the kind of communication that goes on in them.

And not only cities, but also the parts of cities. What planners
call 'zoning' is a useful device for achieving such specialisation;
it means that you limit the forms of communication that are
allowed to take place (devoting an area, for example, to a
shopping centre, or to a university), in order to make that kind

of communication convenient, and to prevent it (or the traffic it generates) interfering with other kinds of communication. Or the total amount of *any* kind of communication that is allowed to take place in a given area can be limited. A wise man in the planning department of Canberra (he was, I think, a disciple of Professor Doxiadis) said to me, 'When we are planning an area, we work out how much the roads will carry, and we don't allow more building and more activities to take place in the area than will generate that amount of traffic'. If this rule had been followed in all cities (it has had lip-service paid to it in many) how much happier they would be!

But once one starts to zone a city – or once it starts zoning itself naturally, as often happens – a great danger emerges. The price of specialisation is isolation. In making it easy for members of parliament to communicate with members of parliament, or businessmen with businessmen, we make it more difficult for them to communicate with other sorts of people. If cities get too segregated – one area for the rich, another for the poor, one for government, another for the governed – then, certainly, communication between one rich man and another rich man, or between one member of the governing class and another member of the governing class, will become much easier. And so, for that matter, will be that between one poor man and another in the same poor district. But the rich and the governing class will be talking to one another in a language which the poor do not understand, and the poor will be talking to each other – perhaps talking of revolution – in a language which (terrifyingly) their rulers do not understand.

We must not forget that a city – an organism for communication – has to be a community. A community is a group of people who can communicate with each other. The city, if it is functioning properly, is something which all of them have *in common*. It is *their* city, and the government of the city is in communication with the people who are being governed. If this communication is cut off, then nobody should be surprised if, in order to re-establish it – to make themselves heard – the governed resort to violence. That, at least, gets them into the newspapers, which their rulers read; so communication is to that extent re-established. Often the rulers, fearing violence, provoke or even start it; for they too have lost the ability to communicate in any other way with those whom they are trying to govern. A community in which violence is the only channel of communication between the ruled and the rulers is a very unhappy one. But it is happier than if there were no communication at all. If Washington were an all-white city, the United States would be worse governed.

How can communication be re-established or preserved otherwise than by violence? How can the city be made into a community? Success in communication is making oneself understood, and understanding what the other person is saying. The instrument of communication is language, and this is what we have to learn. It is much easier now than it was, to *hear* what other people are saying, because of the so-called mass-communication media (the press and radio and television). We *hear* each other by means of communications satellites. But do we always *understand* one another? Do we know each other's languages? Does the Englishman or the American understand what the Hindi speaker is trying to say to him, even when it is translated into English? The mass media can help us to understand, because if one goes on talking, and talking in the right way (argument and explanation, not rhetoric and propaganda), and if, more important still, one goes on listening, one may in the end learn the other person's language. We are beginning to conquer illiteracy. If people can read, they may begin to understand; and even if they cannot read, they may understand what they hear on the radio. But if those who control the radio are trying, for example, to stop the Arabs understanding the Israelis, it might be better if there were no radio at all. The right motto for those in charge of these means of communication is, 'Nation shall speak peace unto nation'. The 'nations' may be those which share and divide a single country or city – rich and poor, black and white. And one cannot speak peace without learning to understand the language of peace.

The key to successful communication, in cities as elsewhere, is understanding; and the key to understanding is education. Education means, or at least always involves, learning to understand a language – for example, the language of mathematics, of science, of democratic politics. Once the language is understood, there is little more to be learnt. The discipline which has as its task the furthering of this understanding is called philosophy; it seeks out the most difficult concepts in our language – the ones which tie us into the biggest knots – and tries to elucidate them so that the knots can be unravelled. The job of philosophy is the clarification of what is obscure in language (little as you would think it, to hear some philosophers talk). A philosopher can perhaps make a small, but essential, contribution to the success of our conference, by beginning the elucidation of what is sure to be its central theme: communication. The conference will be successful to the extent that we manage to communicate with one another about communication between people in cities.

Postscript[1]

What then is this language of peace which we have to understand if we are to live at peace in cities? It is the language of morality, and the language of love. To think that love and morality have different languages, so that the one can be at variance with the other, is a mistake often made by those to whom love means sex, and morality means a book of rules the reasons for which everyone has forgotten. But in truth morality *is* love. For the essence of morality is to treat the interests of others as of equal weight with one's own. Its supreme principle, as Bentham saw, is that everybody is to count as one and nobody as more than one. This means that in making moral decisions we have always to say to ourselves:

> Momentous to himself as I to me
> Is every man that ever women bore.

Only so shall we be able, as Kant put it, to will the maxim of our action to be universal law. But this is also the rule of love, that as we wish that men should do to us, so we should do to them. This is what it is to love our neighbour as ourself.

In the modern city, hate between rich and poor, rulers and ruled, is much easier to preach than love; but unless love is both preached and most skilfully practised, our cities will fall apart.

[1] This was added after the conference.